LEARNING FOR LIFE AND WORK
HOME ECONOMICS IN CLOSE-UP

COLOURPOINT EDUCATIONAL

Laura McGreevy

© Laura McGreevy and Colourpoint Creative Ltd 2015

ISBN: 978-1-78073-089-9

First Edition
Second Impression, 2017

Layout and design: April Sky Design, Newtownards
Printed by: W&G Baird Ltd, Antrim

Laura McGreevy graduated from the University of Ulster in 2007 with a First class honours in Consumer Studies. Within her first year of teaching she was appointed as Head of Department in St Columbanus' College. She has worked with an examining body in a number of different roles, most recently when she was involved in writing the specification for GCSE Entry Level Home Economics and the resources to accompany it.

All rights reserved. No part of this publication may be reproduced, stored in a retrieval system or transmitted in any form or by any means, electronic, mechanical, photocopying, scanning, recording or otherwise, without the prior written permission of the copyright owners and publisher of this book.

Copyright has been acknowledged to the best of our ability. If there are any inadvertent errors or omissions, we shall be happy to correct them in any future editions.

Page 91 constitutes an extension of this copyright page.

Acknowledgements

Thank you to Rachel Irwin at Colourpoint for her guidance in recent months. I always appreciated her approach and how she delivered her feedback, it was always with such warmth and encouragement. Thank you also to Claire Miskelly and Allison Lindsay for taking the time to provide such valuable guidance.

Thanks to my wonderful pupils at St Columbanus' College, who have inspired so much of this book because of their infectious enthusiasm and love towards Home Economics.

Finally, a special thanks to my husband, family and friends for their continued support and encouragement. I dedicate this book to my Dad with love.

Colourpoint Educational
An imprint of Colourpoint Creative Ltd
Colourpoint House
Jubilee Business Park
21 Jubilee Road
Newtownards
County Down
Northern Ireland
BT23 4YH

Tel: 028 9182 0505
Fax: 028 9182 1900
E-mail: sales@colourpoint.co.uk
Web site: www.colourpointeducational.com

Contents

Healthy Eating

1. Hygiene and safety ... 8
2. Equipment ... 10
3. Food storage ... 12
4. Food preparation methods ... 14
5. Cooking methods ... 16
6. Food poisoning ... 18
7. Leftover food ... 20
8. The Eatwell Guide ... 22
9. Eight tips for making healthier choices ... 24
10. Breakfast ... 25
11. Fat ... 27
12. Sugar ... 28
13. Fibre ... 30
14. Water ... 32
15. Modifying recipes ... 34
16. Nutrition through life ... 36
17. Vegetarianism ... 38
18. Food allergies and intolerances ... 40
19. Osteoporosis ... 42
20. Iron deficiency anaemia ... 44
21. Obesity ... 46
22. Coronary heart disease ... 48
23. Factors affecting our food choice ... 49
24. Food around the world ... 51
25. Labelling ... 52

Independent Living

26. Consumerism ... 56
27. Responsible consumers ... 57
28. Factors that influence consumers ... 58
29. Different types of food production ... 60
30. Shopping options ... 62
31. Online shopping ... 64
32. Budgeting ... 66
33. Super savers ... 68
34. Methods of payment ... 70
35. Legislation ... 71
36. Making a complaint ... 74
37. Consumer organisations ... 76

Home and Family Life

38. Different types of families ... 80
39. Roles and responsibilities ... 81
40. Dealing with conflict ... 83
41. Parenting ... 84
42. Changing needs of family members ... 86

Introduction

This book has been written to cover the theory for all three years of Home Economics at Key Stage 3 level. The content addresses:

- all of the **Statutory Requirements** outlined by the Northern Ireland Curriculum.
- the **Cross-curricular Skills, Thinking Skills and Personal Capabilities** required by the Northern Ireland Curriculum.
- the **Core Competences** identified by the British Nutrition Foundation, Public Health England (PHE), Food Standards Agency Northern Ireland, Food Standards Agency Scotland and the Welsh Government.

The book is arranged logically, looking at the three Key Concepts of Healthy Eating, Independent Living and Home and Family Life in order. These concepts are divided into individual chapters, each exploring a different topic and containing activities appropriate for a range of ages and abilities. The stand-alone nature of each chapter means that teachers can choose the most appropriate order to progress through the material during the course of three years.

Core competences

Core Competence boxes are used at the beginning of relevant chapters to show where a core competence for children and young people aged 5 to 16 years is addressed.

> **CORE COMPETENCE** *Example*
> By the age of 14 pupils should..."plan and carry out food storage, preparation and cooking safely and hygienically."

They represent core skills and knowledge around the themes of:

- Diet (food and drink)
- Consumer Awareness
- Cooking (food preparation and handling skills)
- Food Safety
- Active Lifestyles (physical activity)

These competences were developed by the British Nutrition Foundation, Public Health England (PHE), Food Standards Agency Northern Ireland, Food Standards Agency Scotland and the Welsh Government. The full competences framework can be accessed from the British Nutrition Foundation website: http://www.nutrition.org.uk/foodinschools/competences/competences.html

Skills and capabilities key

Icons are used in the text to show where an activity uses the Cross-curricular Skills, Thinking Skills and Personal Capabilities required by the Northern Ireland Curriculum for Key Stage 3.

CROSS-CURRICULAR SKILLS

- 🍎 COM Communication
- 🍎 ICT Using ICT
- 🍎 MA   Using Mathematics

THINKING SKILLS AND PERSONAL CAPABILITIES

- 🍏 WO   Working with Others
- 🍏 MI   Managing Information
- 🍏 SM   Self-management
- 🍏 TPD Thinking, Problem-solving, Decision-making
- 🍏 BC   Being Creative

HOME ECONOMICS
HEALTHY EATING

HEALTHY EATING

1. Hygiene and safety

We are learning about:
- Hygiene and safety rules
- Potential risks in a Home Economics lesson
- What to do if an accident occurs during a lesson

CORE COMPETENCE
By the age of 14 pupils should…"plan and carry out food storage, preparation and cooking safely and hygienically."

As we learn how to prepare and cook foods in our Home Economics classes we are developing skills that we will use throughout our lives. These skills will help us to become more independent. We also need to learn about the health and safety rules to keep our lessons safe and reduce the risk of harm or injury. As our confidence grows we can start to plan our own dishes and take greater responsibility for risk assessing our practical work.

Hygiene and safety rules

Personal hygiene rules
- Wash hands thoroughly before preparing food.
- Remove all jewellery.
- Cover cuts with a blue waterproof plaster.
- Wear a clean apron.
- Tie long hair back.

Safety rules
- Always walk during practical lessons – do not run.
- Place school bags neatly outside the door or in a suitable storage area.
- Wipe up spilt liquids immediately.
- Carry sharp knives by the handle and pointed down towards the floor.
- Make sure that saucepan handles face inwards.
- Have a pot stand ready for placing hot objects on.
- Wear a pair of oven gloves when removing hot food from the oven.
- All equipment must be put away in the correct place.
- Report any breakages to your teacher.

Kitchen hygiene rules
- Tea towels and dishcloths must be clean before use.
- Always make sure utensils and equipment are clean before use.
- Spray tables with antibacterial spray and ensure they are clean and dry before preparing food.
- Use separate chopping boards for raw and cooked meat.

Potential risks in a Home Economics lesson

It is important that we think about the potential risks involved during our practical lessons. We should highlight any potential hazards and suggest actions to prevent any accidents.

Risk assessment

This is the process of:
- identifying any risks or potential hazards involved within a practical lesson.
- suggesting actions that should be taken to reduce these risks.
- recording this information for future reference.

ACTIVITY…
Look at the 'Kitchen Hazards' illustration opposite and identify any potential risks and hazards.

EXTENSION ACTIVITY…
Think of a recent practical lesson and the potential risks involved during it.

Make a copy of the table below and complete it by:
- Outlining each risk.
- Suggesting any actions that could have minimised each risk.
- Adding any additional information.

Use the example below to help you.

RISK	ACTIONS TO MINIMISE RISK	ADDITIONAL INFORMATION
Cutting myself with a sharp knife.	Take extra care when using sharp knives. Point sharp knives down towards the floor and walk slowly.	Use the appropriate knife depending on what ingredients I am preparing, eg vegetable knife or bread knife.

HYGIENE AND SAFETY

Kitchen Hazards

Source: 2008 Flora 'Cooking With Schools' promotion pack. Reproduced with kind permission of Unilever PLC and group companies

THINK ABOUT…
What would you do if an accident occurred in class? Ask your teacher about the school's procedures for dealing with accidents or injuries.

What to do if an accident occurs during a lesson

It is important that we learn some basic first aid information so that we can take greater responsibility for each other and ourselves. If an accident occurs in class we should:

- remain calm.
- report the accident immediately to the teacher.
- seek medical attention if required.

ACTIVITY…
- Where is the first aid box in your classroom?
- Make a list of the items it contains.

Burns and scalds

Burns and scalds are two of the most common kitchen injuries. The first aid advice opposite explains how to treat them.

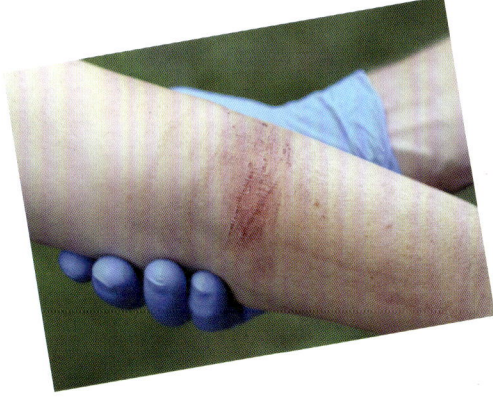

FIRST AID ADVICE

What is the difference between a burn and a scald?
A burn is caused by dry heat, for example touching a grill. A scald is caused by moist heat such as steam from a kettle. The information below from St John Ambulance explains how to treat a burn or scald.

If you think someone has a burn or scald, there are five key things to look for:

- Red skin
- Swelling
- Blisters may form on the skin later on
- The skin may peel
- The skin may be white or scorched

What you need to do:

- Stop the burning getting any worse, by moving the casualty away from the source of heat.
- Start cooling the burn as quickly as possible.
- Run it under cool water for about ten minutes or until the pain feels better. (Don't use ice, creams or gels – they can damage tissues and increase risk of infection).

Assess how bad the burn is.

It is serious if it is:

- larger than the size of the casualty's hand
- on the face, hands or feet.
- a deep burn (the skin turns red and blotchy).

If it is serious, call 999 for emergency medical help.

Source: St John Ambulance, http://www.sja.org.uk

HEALTHY EATING

2. Equipment

We are learning about:
- The different pieces of equipment we may use
- How to use equipment safely

CORE COMPETENCE
By the age of 14 pupils should "use equipment safely, being aware of others' safety."

We will use a wide range of equipment during our study of Home Economics. Some pieces may be completely new to you or your classmates, so it is important we learn how to use the equipment safely. We also need to take responsibility for the equipment, making sure it is clean before use, and cleaned and returned for the next student to use.

Often equipment has more than one use, so we will learn how to be flexible in our approach to using it. For example, spoons are often used for stirring but they can also be used to measure food quickly.

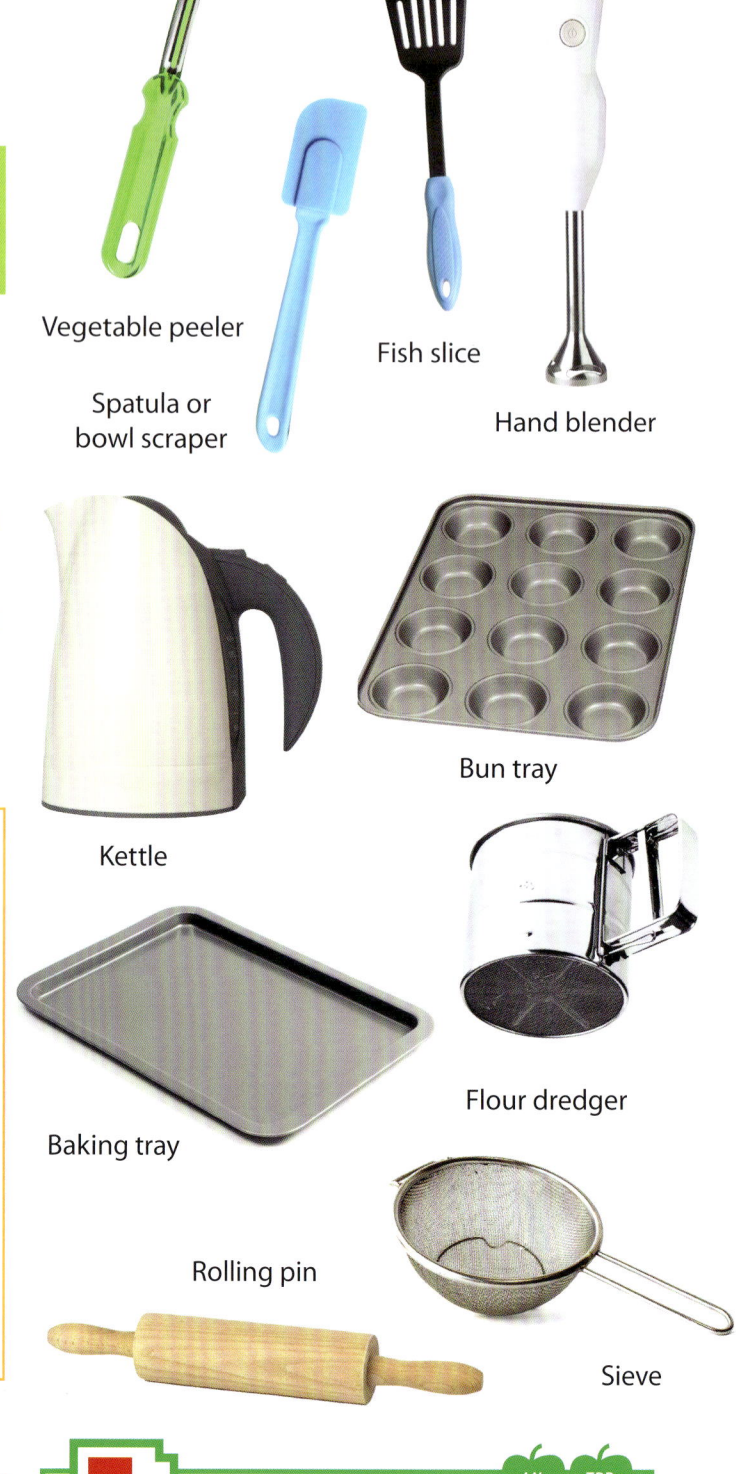

Vegetable peeler

Spatula or bowl scraper

Fish slice

Hand blender

Kettle

Bun tray

Baking tray

Flour dredger

Rolling pin

Sieve

For dry ingredients (eg flour):
- 1 level tablespoon is the equivalent to 15 grams.
- 1 heaped tablespoon is approximately 25 grams.
- 1 level teaspoon is the equivalent to 5 grams.

ACTIVITY...
Take a look around your classroom and make a list of all the different equipment you can see.

ACTIVITY...
State a use for each piece of equipment shown here. If relevant, include a tip for how to use each piece of equipment safely.

EQUIPMENT

ACTIVITY...
What pieces of equipment have you used before and what did you use them for?

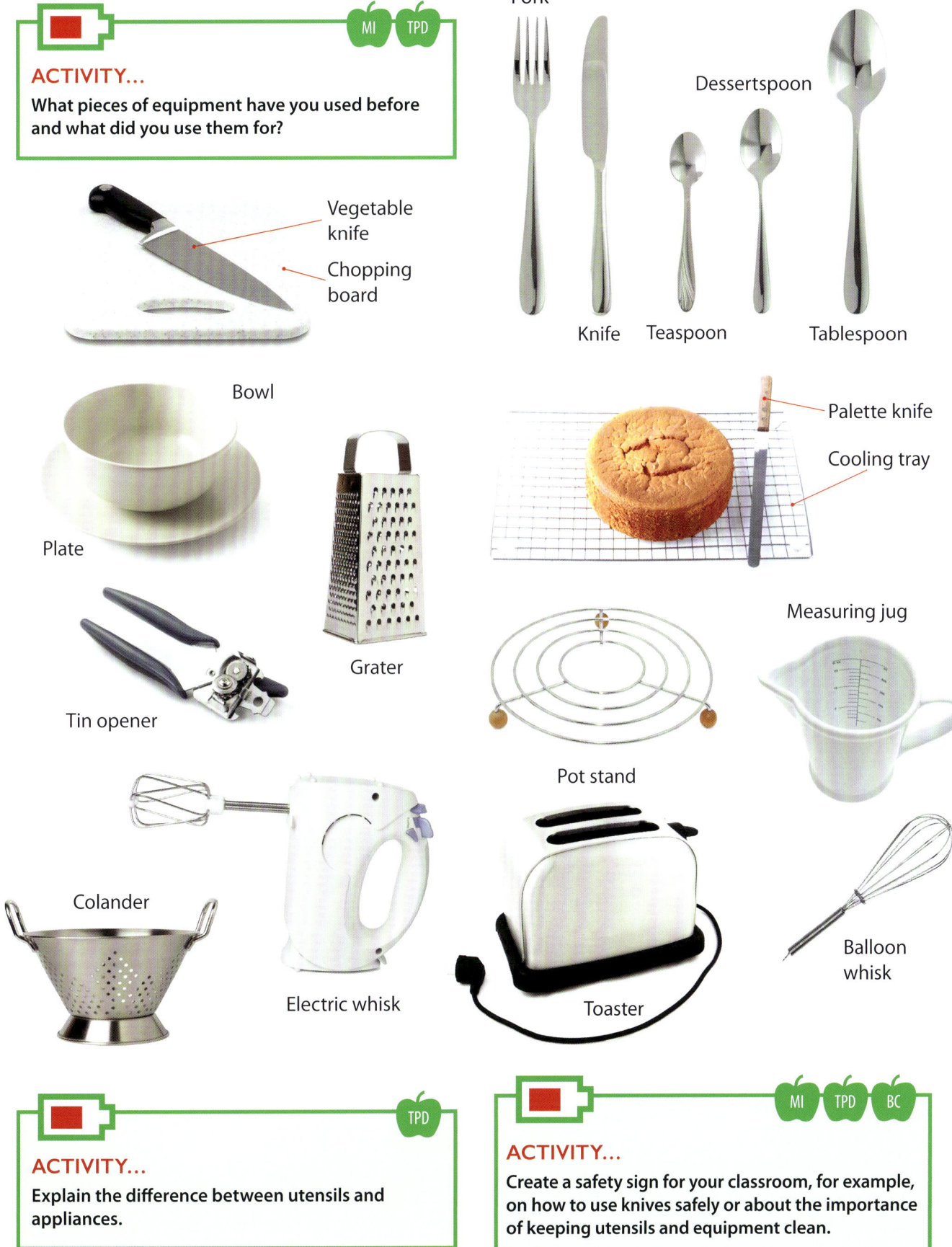

ACTIVITY...
Explain the difference between utensils and appliances.

ACTIVITY...
Create a safety sign for your classroom, for example, on how to use knives safely or about the importance of keeping utensils and equipment clean.

HEALTHY EATING

3. Food storage

We are learning about:
- Different storage options for food
- The difference between 'use-by', 'best before' and 'display until' dates on food

CORE COMPETENCE
By the age of 14 pupils should… "use date-mark and storage instructions when storing and using food and drinks".

It is important we learn about the different storage options for food so that we can choose the most appropriate way to keep our food safe and prevent food poisoning. Before we learn about storage options we need to know a bit about the different types of food.

Types of food

Perishables – These foods go 'off' or 'spoil' quickly (eg meat, fish, poultry and dairy products).

Dried – These foods have had their moisture removed (eg coffee, raisins or stock cubes).

Tinned – These foods are sealed in an airtight container (eg soup, beans or chopped tomatoes).

Frozen – These foods are frozen from fresh or once prepared (eg frozen vegetables and chips).

Pre-prepared and convenience – These foods require little preparation (eg salads, sandwiches, jars of sauce and cook-chill foods such as ready meals). The majority are processed.

Fresh fruit and vegetables – These foods have not been altered or preserved (eg oranges, carrots and tomatoes).

Food storage options
There are many different food storage options to choose from. Some of the most common storage areas are listed in the table opposite, along with examples of the foods suitable to keep there.

Storage	Suitable foods
Fridge Temperature: below 5 °C	Milk, Meat
Freezer Temperature: -18 °C	Frozen peas, Ice cream
Kitchen cupboard/ larder	Tins of soup, Pasta
Fruit bowl	Fruit
Bread bin	Bread, Pancakes

FOOD STORAGE

Where should we store our food in the fridge?
To reduce the risk of food poisoning we must follow some guidelines on how to store our food in the fridge safely. These guidelines will reduce the risk of germs spreading or contaminating our food.

Temperature
The fridge should always be kept below 5 °C. This prevents the bacteria that causes food poisoning from growing and multiplying. You will learn more about this in Chapter 6.

Top and middle shelves
Ready to eat foods (such as milk, cooked meats and sandwiches)

Bottom shelf
Raw meat, poultry or fish (should be covered or sealed)

Salad Drawer
Fruit and vegetables (ideally washed and stored in an airtight container)

THINK ABOUT...
Why is it important that we follow advice about where foods should be stored in the fridge?

ACTIVITY...
Suggest your 3 top tips for how foods should be stored in the fridge.

EXTENSION ACTIVITY...
Create a manual for a student who is moving into his/her own house for the first time.
Advise them on the importance of correctly:
- handling food
- preparing food
- storing food

You might find it useful to illustrate your manual with images or drawings.

Dates on food
There are three main dates that appear on food labels:

Best before – This date relates to the quality of the food. The product will be at its best until this date, after which it may lose its flavour. This date is found on a wide range of food such as dried, frozen and tinned foods.

Use by – This date relates to the safety of the food. The food may be unsafe to eat after this date (unless it is suitable for freezing), so it is important to follow this advice. It is usually found on meat or dairy products.

Display until – This date often appears next to the best before or use by dates. The date provides instructions for staff in the food business to help with stock rotation.

ACTIVITY...
- Look at the range of food products in your house.
- Select 5 examples of foods with different dates on their labels. Record the dates and their type (eg best before, use by or display until).

HEALTHY EATING

4. Food preparation methods

We are learning about:
• A range of methods used for preparing foods

> **CORE COMPETENCE**
> By the age of 14 pupils should... "use a broad range of preparation techniques and methods when cooking."

We will develop a wide range of practical cookery skills during our study of Home Economics. In this chapter we will learn about a range of preparation techniques.

Chopping – is simply cutting food into smaller pieces. We often chop onions, carrots and other fruit and vegetables.

Slicing – is similar to cutting but the pieces are generally cut into thinner sections (eg lemon slices).

Peeling – is the removal of the outer layer of skin from a food (eg a potato or an apple).

Creaming – is the process of combining or blending an ingredient (eg sugar) together with fat (eg butter). We often use this method to make cookie dough or cake mixtures.

Whisking – is the rapid beating or stirring of ingredients (eg eggs or cream) using a whisk. Whisking adds air to the ingredients, causing them to increase in volume.

Sieving – passes ingredients (eg flour) through small holes in a sieve to remove or break down larger pieces and add air.

FOOD PREPARATION METHODS

Rubbing-in – is the rubbing of flour into fat (eg butter) with our fingertips. We often use this method for preparing pastry and scones.

Grating – is the rubbing of food against a grater to shave off small pieces. We often use this method for preparing cheese.

Rolling – is the flattening or spreading of food using a rolling pin. We often use this method for preparing dough for pastry or scones.

EXTENSION ACTIVITY...

Select 1 of the techniques needed to prepare your favourite recipe.

Choose 1 of the following to demonstrate this skill to your class:
- Take photos of the skill and display them on a classroom poster.
- Record a video of the skill and upload it to your school website.

ACTIVITY...

Evaluation skills

Keep a log of your skills throughout your Home Economics course.

You should include:
- The date(s) you learned the skill.
- The name of the dish you made.
- A photograph of the dish.
- What you were good at.
- What you found difficult.
- What you would do differently next time.

PRACTICAL

Plan 1 of the following dishes:
- A fruit crumble using the rubbing-in method for your topping.
- A coleslaw using a range of preparation methods.

ACTIVITY...

Choose 1 of your favourite recipes and write down the techniques needed to prepare the dish.

HEALTHY EATING

5. Cooking methods

We are learning about:
- A range of cooking methods
- How different methods affect the nutritional value of our food

> **CORE COMPETENCE**
> By the age of 14 pupils should… "use a broad range of preparation techniques and methods when cooking, eg stir-frying, steaming and blending."

Cooking transforms food by applying heat to it. We have so many options to choose from when it comes to cooking our food. Something as simple as chicken can be prepared and cooked in many different ways depending on our skills and the utensils, equipment and appliances available to us. Cooking methods can be divided into two main categories:

1. Dry heat cooking methods transfer heat to food items without using any moisture.

2. Moist heat cooking methods transfer heat to food items using moisture, such as steam, water, wine or stock.

Loss of Nutrients

Vitamins
Some vitamins are destroyed through cooking and lose their nutritional value, such as vitamins B and C.

Minerals
There is limited mineral loss in foods during cooking.

Dry heat cooking methods

Grilling
This is when a dry, intense heat is applied directly to food. It is commonly used for meat and for toast.

When we place cheese on toast under the grill the cheese melts and changes colour (from pale yellow to golden brown).

Baking
This cooking method uses prolonged dry heat. Foods such as bread, cakes and cookies are baked in an oven.

Roasting
This method of cooking involves cooking foods in a hot oven. The hot air envelops the food, cooking it evenly on all sides.

Moist heat cooking methods

Stir-frying
This is a quick method of cooking, originating from China, which cooks food in a hot wok. It is popular for cooking vegetables and it is an excellent way of retaining nutrients.

Steaming
This cooking method uses boiling water to produce steam, which in turn cooks our food. It is a very healthy method of cooking vegetables quickly.

COOKING METHODS

Boiling
This method cooks food in a saucepan of boiling water.

Simmering
This method cooks food in a liquid just below boiling point. It is more gentle that boiling.

Stewing
This method is used to boil or simmer meat slowly, usually in a covered pan or a slow cooker. The liquid the food is cooked in tenderises the meat and the flavours in the dish develop.

Poaching
This method cooks food in a liquid such as water, milk or stock at a lower temperature than boiling or simmering.

ACTIVITY...
There are lots of different ways to cook eggs. List as many cooking methods as you can think of.

RESEARCH ACTIVITY...
- Research the methods of cooking in the table opposite.
- Make a copy of the table and complete it by describing how each cooking method works and listing examples of foods that can be cooked in this way.

Methods of cooking	Description	Examples of foods
Frying		
Steaming		
Boiling		
Stewing		
Roasting		
Grilling		
Barbecuing		

PRACTICAL
Prepare an egg in 1 of the following ways: fried, poached, boiled or scrambled.

17

HEALTHY EATING

6. Food poisoning

We are learning about:
- What food poisoning is
- The causes and the symptoms
- How to prevent food poisoning
- Food hygiene ratings

> **CORE COMPETENCE**
> By the age of 14 pupils should… "understand that some foods have a higher risk of food poisoning than others, eg raw chicken".

We will handle a wide range of ingredients in our Home Economics classes and throughout our lives, so we need to take responsibility for our food safety. Food safety is all about keeping food safe during preparation, cooking and storage, with the aim of preventing the contamination that leads to food poisoning. It is important we learn about food safety and proper food hygiene so we can reduce our risk of food poisoning.

What is food poisoning?
Food poisoning occurs when a person becomes ill after eating contaminated food.

The causes
Food poisoning is caused by eating contaminated food. Bacteria may have contaminated the food at any stage of production, processing or cooking. Here are some examples of how food may become contaminated:

- Not cooking food properly (eg meat).
- Cross-contamination (where bacteria spreads between food, surfaces and equipment).
- Not storing food properly.
- Not handling food hygienically.

Bacteria will grow and multiply depending on four conditions:

1. **Food** (bacteria need energy to grow and this energy comes from food)
2. **Time** (bacteria need time to multiply)
3. **Moisture** (bacteria need water to grow and will die without a water source)
4. **Heat** (bacteria grow rapidly between 5–63 °C, known as the 'danger zone')

When the conditions are right, bacteria reproduce by dividing into two about every 20–30 minutes. Just one bacteria cell can produce millions of bacteria in the space of 24 hours.

The symptoms
- Vomiting
- Diarrhoea
- Fever
- Stomach pains
- Headache

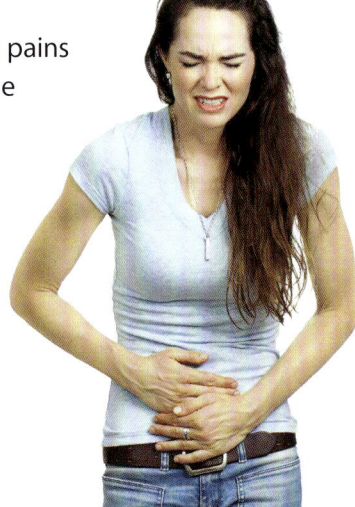

Foods that may cause food poisoning
Foods that are more likely to cause food poisoning than others are called 'high risk'. These include:

- Meat and poultry
- Pâté
- Seafood and shellfish
- Cooked rice and pasta
- Egg based products
- Dairy, fresh cream or milk based products

Types of food poisoning
There are many different types of food poisoning, including salmonella, listeria and staphylococcus aureus.

FOOD POISONING

RESEARCH ACTIVITY...
Research the following types of food poisoning:
- Salmonella
- Listeria
- Staphylococcus aureus

Make a copy of the table opposite and use your research to complete it.

TPD · MI · SM · ICT

Type of food poisoning	Symptoms	Food associated with this type	How to prevent it
Salmonella			
Listeria			
Staphylococcus aureus			

How to prevent food poisoning
- Wash hands properly before and after preparing food.
- Use separate chopping boards when preparing raw and ready to eat food.
- Cook food thoroughly.
- Store raw meat correctly in the fridge (on the bottom shelf).
- Follow the 'use by' date on the packaging.

 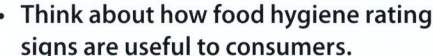 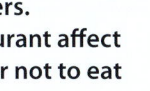

THINK ABOUT...
- Think about how food hygiene rating signs are useful to consumers.
- Would the rating of a restaurant affect your decision on whether or not to eat there?

MI · TPD

Food hygiene ratings

Have you ever noticed the stickers on restaurant, café and food establishment doors that give a food hygiene rating? According to the Food Standards Agency, the food hygiene rating or inspection result given to a business (rated 0–5) reflects the standards of food hygiene found on the date of inspection. It is not a guide to the quality of the food.

ACTIVITY...
Find out the hygiene rating of your school canteen.

MI · TPD

RESEARCH ACTIVITY...
Research 5 different food establishments.
- Record their ratings and when they were inspected.
- Comment on your findings.

MI · TPD · COM · ICT

HEALTHY EATING

7. Leftover food

We are learning about:
- Common examples of leftover food
- How to make use of leftover food safely
- How to reduce the amount of leftover food we have

CORE COMPETENCE
By the age of 14 pupils should… "know how to safely make use of leftovers".

When following a recipe we generally use the quantities it suggests. This often means we have leftover ingredients, such as a bit of onion or half a jar of sauce, and it is all too easy to throw them in the bin. Just think about how much food is wasted in this way and how much money we could save if we made use of our leftover ingredients. That is why it is important we learn how to creatively and safely make use of our leftovers.

THINK ABOUT…
Consider all the factors (reasons) why some people waste food.

DID YOU KNOW?
According to Love Food Hate Waste, the UK throws away 15 million tonnes of waste each year. 7 million tonnes of this is household waste and most of it is food that could have been eaten!

Below are some examples of the amount and cost of food wasted in the UK every year:

Food wasted	Amount	Cost
Home made & pre-prepared meals	440,000 tonnes	£2,100,000,000
Bread	460,000 tonnes	£550,000,000

Source: Figures from Love Food Hate Waste Northern Ireland, http://ni.lovefoodhatewaste.com

RESEARCH ACTIVITY…
Use the Internet to research some up-to-date facts and figures about the cost of food waste in the UK each year. The following website might help you:

Love Food Hate Waste – http://ni.lovefoodhatewaste.com

Common examples of leftover food

Vegetables – Leftover vegetables can be added to dishes to improve the nutritional quality. Vegetables that are past their display date but still safe to eat can be used to make soup.

Potatoes – Potatoes that are already cooked can be used in so many ways the following day. For example, mashed potato can be used on cottage pie or in fish cakes, new potatoes can be used to make a potato salad and fried potatoes are a delicious way of using leftover potato.

Bread – Leftover bread can be used to make bread and butter pudding. Bread that is past its use by date but without any signs of mould can be used to make breadcrumbs.

Pasta – Pasta that is already cooked can be used to make pasta salad. There are so many different types

LEFTOVER FOOD

of pasta salads, be creative and experiment with some recipes!

Rice – Cooked rice can be used the next day in salads or can be fried and added to meat or vegetables to create our own special fried rice.

Meat – Cooked meat can be used the next day for a sandwich filling, on a salad, to top a pizza or inside a savoury dish.

ACTIVITY...
Choose 1 of the following leftover cooked ingredients:
- Potatoes
- Pasta
- Rice

List as many dishes as you can think of that you could prepare using this ingredient.

How to use leftover food safely

Leftover food must be stored and prepared safely to avoid food poisoning. The following guidelines will help keep leftover food safe to eat:

Cooling – Leftover cooked food should be cooled as quickly as possible.

Storing – Once cooled, it should be stored in an airtight container in the fridge or frozen immediately. Bacteria grows at room temperature, so the sooner the food is refrigerated or frozen, the lower the risk of food poisoning. Caution is also needed when reheating rice as it can contain harmful toxins.

Storage times – Leftover food storage times vary from food to food but in general leftover cooked food should not be stored in the fridge for more than 2–3 days or in the freezer for more than 2–3 months.

Reheating – Leftovers should be reheated until they are piping hot the whole way through. This will destroy some of the bacteria that cause food poisoning.

Thawing – Leftover food that has been stored in the freezer should be thawed in the fridge. This is the safest way to thaw leftovers.

Meal planning

The more detailed our meal planning is the less likely we are to waste food. It is a good idea to plan our meals for the week ahead and write a shopping list of the ingredients we need. If we discover that we are using the same ingredient more than once that week, we can modify our recipes to reduce the potential waste. For example, if we plan to make spaghetti bolognese on a Monday and require 2 onions, we might decide to save ½ an onion to make a coleslaw or top a pizza on the Tuesday.

ACTIVITY...
Choose 1 of the following leftover unprepared ingredients:
- Half an onion
- Half a red pepper
- 200 g of grated cheese

List as many dishes as you can think of that you could prepare using this ingredient.

HEALTHY EATING

8. The Eatwell Guide

We are learning about:
- Advice related to healthy eating
- Taking greater responsibility for our health
- The different sections within the Eatwell Guide
- Composite foods

> **CORE COMPETENCE**
> By the age of 14 pupils should "…use current healthy eating advice to help them choose a varied balanced diet for their needs and the needs of others."

The Eatwell Guide

The Eatwell Guide was created by the Food Standards Agency to help us understand what makes up a healthy and balanced diet. Presented in a clear, visual format (picture), the Eatwell Guide shows how much of what you eat should come from each food group. This includes everything you eat during the day, including snacks. It is important that we learn about the Eatwell Guide so that we can take greater responsibility for our own health.

The five sections of the Eatwell Guide
- fruit and vegetables
- potatoes, bread, rice, pasta and other starchy carbohydrates
- dairy and alternatives
- beans, pulses, fish, eggs, meat and other proteins
- oils and spreads

ACTIVITY…
Create your own Eatwell Guide. Use a paper plate for the base and illustrate it with your own food drawings or images from magazines or the Internet.

THINK ABOUT…
- What section of the Eatwell Guide is the largest?
- Why is it important for us to include foods from all sections of the Guide within our diet?

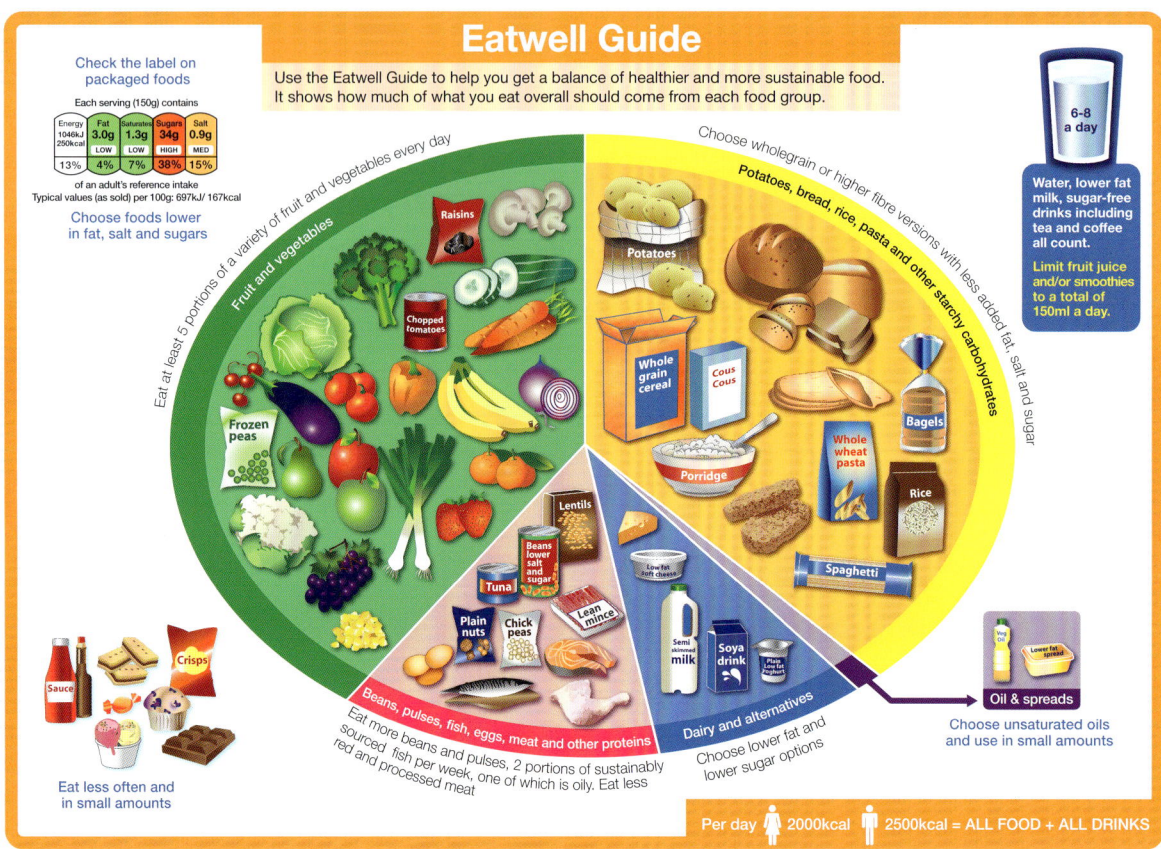

Source: Public Health England in association with the Welsh government, Food Standards Scotland and the Food Standards Agency in Northern Ireland. © Crown copyright 2017. Licensed under the Open Government Licence. A copy of this license can be viewed at: www.nationalarchives.gov.uk/doc/open-government-licence/version/3/

THE EATWELL GUIDE

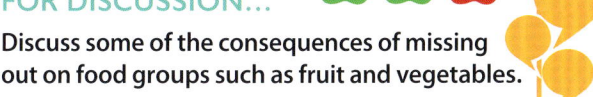

FOR DISCUSSION…
Discuss some of the consequences of missing out on food groups such as fruit and vegetables.

Fruit and vegetables
Fruit and vegetables provide us with essential nutrients that help our bodies fight disease. We should try to include a wide variety and colour of fruit and vegetables in our diet. We are encouraged to eat at least five portions of fruit and vegetables every day but do you know what one portion looks like? Examples include 1 slice of large fruit (eg melon or pineapple), 1 piece of medium sized fruit (eg banana) or 1 cup of small fruit (eg grapes).

Potatoes, bread, rice, pasta and other starchy carbohydrates
Many of us include foods from this group in the majority of our meals. It is important that we include foods such as bread, rice, potatoes and pasta in our diet because they provide us with nutrients such as carbohydrate and fibre. Foods from this group give our bodies the energy we need to function.

Dairy and alternatives
This group includes foods such as milk, yogurt and cheese. These foods are really good for our bones and teeth because they are very high in calcium. They are also high in protein which helps our bodies grow and repair. We are encouraged to eat 3 portions from this food group each day.

Beans, pulses, fish, eggs, meat and other proteins
This group provides us with a range of nutrients, particularly protein. We need protein for growth and repair. Non-dairy sources of protein include foods such as nuts, pulses, Quorn and Tofu.

Oils and spreads
This is the smallest section of the Eatwell Guide. We are encouraged to choose unsaturated oils and us in small amounts.

THINK ABOUT…
- What nutrients are found in each section of the Eatwell Guide?
- How does the Eatwell Guide help us make healthier food choices?

Composite foods
The word 'composite' means 'made up of several parts'. What do you think the term 'composite food' means? In this context, it simply means a food or dish made up of different sections of the Eatwell Guide. A Shepherd's Pie and pizza could be described as composite foods because they include several sections from the Eatwell Guide.

INGREDIENTS	FOOD GROUP
Potatoes	Potatoes, bread, rice, pasta and other starchy carbohydrates
Mince	Beans, pulses, fish, eggs, meat and other proteins
Cheese	Dairy and alternatives
Onions	Fruit and vegetables
Carrots	Fruit and vegetables
Peas	Fruit and vegetables

ACTIVITY…
- List 5 foods from each group of the Eatwell Guide.
- Think of 3 composite foods and identify the food group each ingredient relates to.

RESEARCH ACTIVITY…
Research different healthy eating models and guidance from around the world.

Present your research as a report or PowerPoint presentation. Your report/presentation should:
- Identify the strengths and weaknesses for each model.
- Make suggestions as to how they could be improved.
- Comment on how useful you think each model is.

PRACTICAL
Plan a healthy composite meal that includes foods from all the sections of the Eatwell Guide.

HEALTHY EATING

9. Eight tips for making healthier choices

We are learning about:
- Advice related to healthy eating
- The 8 tips for making healthier choices
- Taking greater responsibility for our health

CORE COMPETENCE
By the age of 14 pupils should "…use current healthy eating advice to help them choose a varied balanced diet for their needs and those of others."

Now that we understand the Eatwell Guide, we are going to learn about the other dietary advice that we should follow. The following 8 tips for making healthier choices were created by the Food Standards Agency:

8 TIPS
1. Base your meals on starchy foods.
2. Eat lots of fruit and vegetables.
3. Eat more fish – including a portion of oily fish each week.
4. Cut down on saturated fat and sugar.
5. Try to eat less salt – no more than 6g a day for adults.
6. Get active and try to be a healthy weight.
7. Drink plenty of water.
8. Don't skip breakfast.

ACTIVITY… *Food in our school*
Working in a group, design a questionnaire to assess how closely students your age follow the 8 tips for making healthier choices. Your questionnaire should:

- Include a checklist to see if they follow each tip or not.
- Ask them for examples of the tips that they do follow.
- Ask them to reflect on their choices. (eg What tips do they follow every day? How could they make their lifestyle healthier?)

EXTENSION ACTIVITY…
When the questionnaire is ready you could distribute it amongst your class, year group or even your school. When you have collected the results, you will need to analyse them. Below are some tips on how to analyse results.

- State the results. You might want to present them as graph or pie chart.
- Are the results what you expected or are you surprised by them? Give reasons for your answer.
- Explain the significance of your findings. Why are your results important?

Finally, you could present your findings to your teacher, student council or Principal.

PRACTICAL
Plan a dish that reflects 1 or more of the 8 tips.

BREAKFAST

10. Breakfast

We are learning about:
- The importance of eating breakfast
- Reasons why some people don't eat breakfast
- Breakfast around the world

Breakfast really is the most important meal of the day. Just think about it, your body has been fasting throughout the night, maybe even since dinner time. This could be over 12 hours!

The importance of breakfast

Eating breakfast helps improve our concentration. If we concentrate in school we are likely to learn more and achieve better grades in our subjects. Breakfast also kick starts our metabolism and gives us energy. It's like filling a car up with fuel! People who skip breakfast are more likely to eat high energy foods at break time than those who had a healthy breakfast with a good amount of fibre. This is because fibre helps keep us fuller for longer. We will learn more about fibre in Chapter 13.

ACTIVITY...
Suggest 5 healthy breakfast ideas that are suitable for a teenager.

Reasons why some people don't eat breakfast

Did you eat your breakfast this morning? Ask your classmates for a show of hands for those who had breakfast and those who don't. You may be surprised to discover the amount of people who didn't. There are many reasons why some people do not eat breakfast:

- Our time is precious, especially in the mornings! Some people simply do not make the time to include breakfast in their routine.
- Many people just don't feel like eating soon after they get up.
- Some people choose not to eat breakfast because they think it will help them lose weight. This isn't true because people who skip breakfast are more likely to snack before lunch on high energy (and high calorie) foods.

ACTIVITY...

Breakfast survey

Conduct a survey of your class to discover:
- Who eats breakfast and who doesn't.
- What foods are the most popular for breakfast.

EXTENSION ACTIVITY...

Create charts to show the results of your class survey and comment on your findings.

ACTIVITY...
Read the case study below.
- What are the reasons behind Emma's choice to avoid breakfast?
- What problems do you think this could create for Emma? Try to think of a wide range of issues.
- What advice would you give to Emma?

CASE STUDY

"Hi! My name is Emma. Our school disco is soon and my dress doesn't fit so I've decided to lose weight. I have avoided breakfast for the past week now and am becoming a vegetarian. I had to be excused from PE today because my teacher said I looked very tired but what does she know?"

ACTIVITY...
- Do you have a breakfast club in your school? If so, do you go to it?
- How could your school promote their breakfast club and make it more attractive to students? Write down your suggestions.

25

HEALTHY EATING

Breakfast around the world
Many of us have cereal or toast for our breakfast but there are many other breakfast dishes from around the world to choose from. What do you enjoy for breakfast? A bacon sandwich? Fruit and yogurt? Eggs? Have you experienced a breakfast from another country?

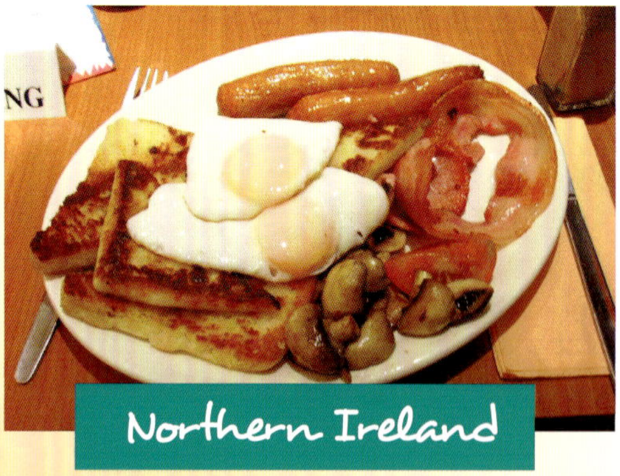

RESEARCH ACTIVITY...
Research breakfasts from 5 different countries.
- Write down a popular breakfast dish from each country.
- How could each breakfast be modified to make it healthier?

THINK ABOUT...
What foods does a continental breakfast include? Can you list some examples?

PRACTICAL
Plan a healthy breakfast.

11. Fat

We are learning about:
- The role of fat in our diet
- Foods that are high in fat
- The different types of fat
- How to reduce our fat intake

> **CORE COMPETENCE**
> By the age of 14 pupils should "…know that food and drinks provide energy and nutrients in different amounts and that they have important functions in the body."

The role of fat in our diet

Although we are advised to reduce the amount of fat we eat, our bodies do need some fat to function properly. We need fat to protect our organs, keep us warm and provide us with energy. Approximately 35% of our energy intake should come from fat. Foods that are high in fat also supply us with fat soluble vitamins.

Foods that are high in fat

Fat is found in the following foods: meat, butter, lard, cooking oil, cakes, biscuits, crisps, fried foods and many processed foods. They all provide us with different types of fat, so we are going to learn about two main types:

Saturated fat is solid at room temperature. It is found mainly in animal foods (eg meat and dairy products) but also other foods (eg cakes and biscuits).

Unsaturated fat is liquid at room temperature. It is found in plant sources such as olive oil and avocados.

Too much saturated fat in our diet is bad for us. It can cause weight gain, obesity and blocked arteries, which can lead to coronary heart disease. We will learn about coronary heart disease in Chapter 22.

ACTIVITY…
What is the difference between saturated and unsaturated fat? List 3 food examples for each.

How to manage our fat intake

What foods do you eat that contain fat? How often do you eat these foods? Knowing where the fat in our diet comes from is an important step towards managing the amount of fat we eat each day.

Below are some other ways to help us reduce our fat intake:

- Choose a healthy method of cooking (eg grilling food instead of frying it).
- Cut visible fat off meat.
- Cut down on the amount of fatty spreads used.
- Choose low fat alternatives of common foods (eg milk and yogurt).
- Read the label, watch out for foods labelled 'lower in fat' or 'light', as their fat content may still be considered high.

We will learn about food labelling in Chapter 25 but make sure you look out for the fat and saturated fat content on the label when you are choosing food and planning meals.

HEALTHY EATING

ACTIVITY...

Create an advertising campaign to help make young people more aware of the fat content of foods they eat. You may want to include information on:

- The fat content of some foods.
- The impact fat has on our health.

12. Sugar

We are learning about:
- The role of sugar in our diet
- Foods that are high in sugar
- Different types of sugar
- Tooth decay and diabetes
- How to reduce our sugar intake

> **CORE COMPETENCE**
> By the age of 14 pupils should "…know that food and drinks provide energy and nutrients in different amounts and that they have important functions in the body."

We are advised to cut down on the amount of sugar we eat. In this section we are going to learn why we shouldn't include too much sugar in our diet, the role sugar plays in our body and the impact it can have on our health.

Different types of sugar

We know that many foods are high in sugar, such as sweets, biscuits, cakes and fizzy drinks. The sugar in these foods and drinks is known as 'visible' sugar, because we know it's there. However, did you know that there are also 'invisible' or 'hidden' sugars? These sugars are often found in canned foods such as tomato soup and baked beans.

There are two main types of sugar found in our diet:

1. **Intrinsic** – these are sugars that are found **naturally** within the cell wall of foods such as fruit.
2. **Extrinsic** – these are sugars which are found outside the cell wall of foods such as milk or honey. These sugars can be divided into:
   - Milk sugars (lactose)
   - Non milk extrinsic sugars (eg confectionery). These sugars are often added to foods via cooking or processing.

PRACTICAL

Plan a healthy dish that replaces high fat ingredients with low fat versions. For example, cheesecake made with low fat biscuits and low fat soft cheese.

SUGAR

Tooth decay

Too much sugar in our diet can lead to tooth decay. Tooth decay occurs when plaque builds up on our teeth causing the outer layer of our tooth to dissolve. You can help prevent tooth decay by:

- Brushing your teeth at least twice a day.
- Avoiding snacking between meals.
- Visiting your dentist regularly.

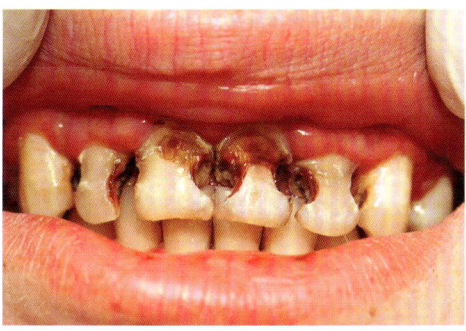

Diabetes

Diabetes is caused when a person's blood sugar levels are too high for too long. This is because the body is not breaking down sugar the way it should. It is a very serious condition and appears to be on the increase. By 2030, the NHS predicts that 4.6 million people will have diabetes, with 90% of those having Type 2 diabetes. There are two different types of diabetes:

> 1. **Type 1** – This type of diabetes occurs when the body isn't able to produce any insulin. It is managed by insulin injections and is more likely to develop in people before the age of 40.
>
> 2. **Type 2** – This type of diabetes occurs when the body produces some insulin but not enough. It is controlled by diet. Unlike Type 1 diabetes, Type 2 often occurs in people over the age of 40.

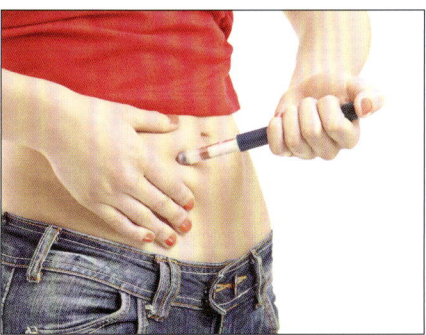

THINK ABOUT...

Why do think the number of people with diabetes is increasing?

How to reduce our sugar intake

Here are some ways to help us reduce our sugar intake:

- Replace high sugar drinks with water.
- Don't add sugar to hot drinks.
- Avoid snacking on high sugar foods between meals. Choose sugar free snacks instead.
- Read the label to check the sugar content within the food.
- Choose reduced sugar foods.
- If buying tinned fruit, choose fruit that is stored in natural juice rather than syrup.

ACTIVITY...

Working in a group, think of 5 foods or drinks that are high in sugar. You might want to include energy drinks to highlight just how high in sugar some of them are!

- Find out how many grams of sugar are in each food per 100 g.
- Record the results and create a bar chart to show your findings.
- Discuss your results and come up with some recommendations on how people your age could reduce their daily sugar intake.

HEALTHY EATING

13. Fibre

We are learning about:
- The importance of fibre in our diet
- Sources of fibre
- How to increase the amount of fibre we eat

> **CORE COMPETENCE**
> By the age of 14 pupils should "…understand the implications of dietary excess or deficiency."

Fibre is also known as non-starch polysaccharide (NSP). It plays a very important role in our body. Adults are advised to have a least 18 g of fibre each day.

The importance of fibre in our diet

A diet high in fibre helps our digestive system (prevents constipation) and can help reduce our risk of developing diabetes, heart disease, obesity and some cancers.

There are two types of fibre:

> **Soluble**
> - Helps reduce the amount of cholesterol in our blood.
> - Helps control blood sugar levels.
>
> **Insoluble**
> - Assists digestion.
> - Prevents constipation.

Sources of fibre

Food	Fibre content (approximate)
1 apple	10.3 g
All-Bran™ (6 tablespoons)	10.3 g
Wholemeal bread (1 slice)	2.1 g
Wholewheat pasta (230 g)	8.1 g
A small tin of baked beans (200 g)	7.4 g

> **THINK ABOUT…**
> Why are baked potatoes in their skin a better source of fibre than creamed potatoes?

How to increase the amount of fibre we eat

- Eat fruit or vegetables as snacks.
- Add vegetables to sauces.
- Add dried fruit to cakes/scones.
- Use wholemeal flour.
- Eat wholegrain breakfast cereals.

FIBRE

ACTIVITY...
- Place 1 Weetabix™ in a bowl and cover it with milk.
- Leave the Weetabix™ in the bowl until the milk has been absorbed.
- Comment on your observations.

EXTENSION ACTIVITY...
Suggest high fibre alternatives to the following:
- A glass of orange juice.
- A vanilla yogurt.
- Macaroni cheese with white pasta.
- Sausage and potato mash.

ACTIVITY...
Read the case studies below.
- Who do you think had a healthier breakfast? Give reasons for your answer.
- What caused Peter to feel so full?
- How could each breakfast be improved?

ACTIVITY...
CLASS DEBATE

Organise a class debate with the motion:

'Juicing is the only way to achieve the recommended amount of fruit and vegetables in our diet.'

Working in groups of 4:
- Research the advantages and disadvantages of
   a) juicing and
   b) eating fruit and vegetables.
- Decide whether your group is for or against the motion.
- Prepare a speech for or against the motion and select a speaker to represent your group to the class.
- Time to debate! Your teacher will select a chairperson to keep order.

CASE STUDY 1
Shauna was given four large oranges to make herself orange juice for breakfast. She made her juice and drank it. She also had some cereal (fortified) with milk for her breakfast.

CASE STUDY 2
Peter was given four large oranges to eat for his breakfast. He ate two full oranges but could only eat a couple of segments of the third orange. He had to stop because he felt so full!

PRACTICAL
Plan 1 of the following dishes:
- Wheaten bread
- Wheaten scones

HEALTHY EATING

14. Water

We are learning about:
- The role of water in our diet
- The water content of some foods
- How to promote water in our school

> **CORE COMPETENCE**
> By the age of 14 pupils should "...know that bodies contain water and that they need fluid from food and drinks to keep the body working properly."

The role of water in our diet

Did you know that water makes up about two thirds of our body weight? Water plays a very important role in helping our body to function properly. Water helps to:

- avoid dehydration.
- transport nutrients around our body.
- get rid of body waste.

Dehydration

Dehydration occurs when our bodies do not have enough water.

Causes: Not drinking enough fluids, sweating during exercise, vomiting or diarrhoea.

Symptoms: Feeling thirsty, dry mouth, headache, tiredness and reduced urine.

How much water should we drink?

The European Food Safety Authority recommends the following:

- Women should drink 1.6 litres of fluid per day.
- Men should drink 2.0 litres of fluid per day.

That's about eight 200 ml glasses for a woman, and ten glasses for a man.

Water content of foods

Although we are advised to drink between 8–10 glasses of water a day, approximately 20% of our water intake comes from solid foods. The table below shows the high water content of some fruit and vegetables.

Food	Water content (approximate)
Cucumber	96 %
Pineapple	95 %
Tomato	94 %
Watermelon	92 %

WATER

RESEARCH ACTIVITY...
Choose 5 fruit and vegetables.
- Research their water content.
- Rank them from the highest to the lowest water content.

EXTENSION ACTIVITY...
- Create a bar chart to present your research about the water content of fruit and vegetables.
- Don't forget to include a title and label your axis.

Promoting water in school

Now that we have learned about the importance of water in our diet we should encourage others in our school to drink more.

FOR DISCUSSION...
How easy is it to get a drink of water in your school?
- Are you allowed to drink water in class?
- Are there water fountains or coolers around the school?
- Do you have to go to the canteen to get water?
- Do you have to pay for water?

THINK ABOUT...
How could you encourage students to drink more throughout the school day?

ACTIVITY...
Design a poster that encourages students to drink more water.

You might want to include information on:
- Why we need to drink water.
- How much water we need each day.
- 5 top tips on how to drink more water throughout the day.

EXTENSION ACTIVITY...
How will you monitor the effectiveness of your poster? Has it made people drink more water or even consider drinking more water?

HEALTHY EATING

15. Modifying recipes

We are learning about:
- Why people modify recipes
- How we can modify recipes to make them healthier

> **CORE COMPETENCE**
> By the age of 14 pupils should…"modify recipes based on current healthy eating messages."

To modify something simply means to make a change to it. There are many reasons why people modify recipes, so it is important we learn about these reasons and how we can change recipes to make them healthier.

Why people modify recipes

Health – Think back to what we have learned about healthy eating and Government advice. In particular reflect on the Eatwell Guide and the 8 tips for healthy eating. We are advised to eat less:

- Sugar
- Fat
- Salt

We are also advised to try and eat more:

- Fibre

ACTIVITY…
- Give 3 reasons why we are advised to cut down our intake of fat, salt and sugar.
- Give 2 reasons why we are advised to increase the amount of fibre we eat.

Personal likes/dislikes – Some recipes might contain ingredients or use a method of cooking that we do not like.

Time – Some recipes can be time consuming. If time is limited, we may decide to use a jar of sauce or packet of grated cheese instead of making our own sauce or grating our own cheese from a block.

Cost – Some ingredients are very expensive and we may not want to spend a lot of money on food. For example, steak can be expensive. A simple modification would be to use a cheaper cut of meat instead.

Quantity – Some recipes are designed for one person and others are designed to feed four. We may decide to change the quantity of the ingredients to cater for the amount of people being served.

Availability of ingredients – Some fruits and vegetables are only available at certain times of the year and others may only be found in specific countries or regions. We might need to pick different ingredients that are available instead.

Skills of the person preparing the recipe – Recipes involve different preparation skills and techniques. If we are unsure about or don't have the skill to complete the recipe, we might decide to modify it to use skills that we do have.

Equipment/utensils available – If a recipe involves using specific equipment or utensils that we don't have, we may decide to modify the recipe to use the equipment and utensils available to us.

Food allergies/intolerances – If we (or the person we are cooking for) have a food allergy or intolerance then we may decide to modify a recipe so that it doesn't include the ingredient that causes a reaction in our bodies.

MODIFYING RECIPES

How can we modify recipes to make them healthier?

We can modify recipes to make them healthier in many different ways. Below are some examples:

Food	Modification
Sugar	Sweetener
Full fat milk	Skimmed milk
Salt	Low salt alternative
White rice	Brown rice

ACTIVITY...

- Give reasons for each of the modifications listed in the table above.
- Suggest 3 ways to reduce our fat, salt and sugar intake.
- Suggest 3 ways to increase the amount of fibre we eat.

ACTIVITY...

Ingredients:
- 500 g mince
- 1 red pepper
- Tin of tomatoes
- 2 tablespoons tomato puree
- 2 cloves of garlic
- ½ onion
- Teaspoon salt
- Tablespoon oil
- 100 g parmesan cheese (sprinkle on top)
- Spaghetti

Suggest 4 healthy changes that could be made to the ingredients list above. Give reasons for your suggestions.

ACTIVITY...

Think of a dish you have prepared recently. Plan this dish again, modifying the recipe in 1 of the following ways:

- Make the dish cost less.
- Make the dish healthier.
- Use a different skill to prepare your dish.
- Change an ingredient to accommodate a person with a food allergy or intolerance.
- Use different utensils or appliances.

HEALTHY EATING

16. Nutrition through life

We are learning about:
- Nutritional needs throughout the human life cycle

> **CORE COMPETENCE**
> By the age of 14 pupils should "…know that food and drinks provide energy in different amounts and that people require different amounts during their life."

Our energy needs and nutritional requirements change throughout life. They depend on:

- Age
- Gender
- Weight
- Level of physical activity

It is important we learn about the nutritional needs for the different stages of our life so we can prevent diet and health related problems. We should also try to follow the advice from the Eatwell Guide and the 8 tips for making healthier choices.

ACTIVITY…
List 5 healthy snacks that children should be encouraged to eat instead of foods high in fat or sugar. Give reasons for your suggestions.

RESEARCH ACTIVITY…
Choose 1 stage of the human life cycle.
- Research the diet related deficiencies common to this stage.
- Record your information as a fact sheet.

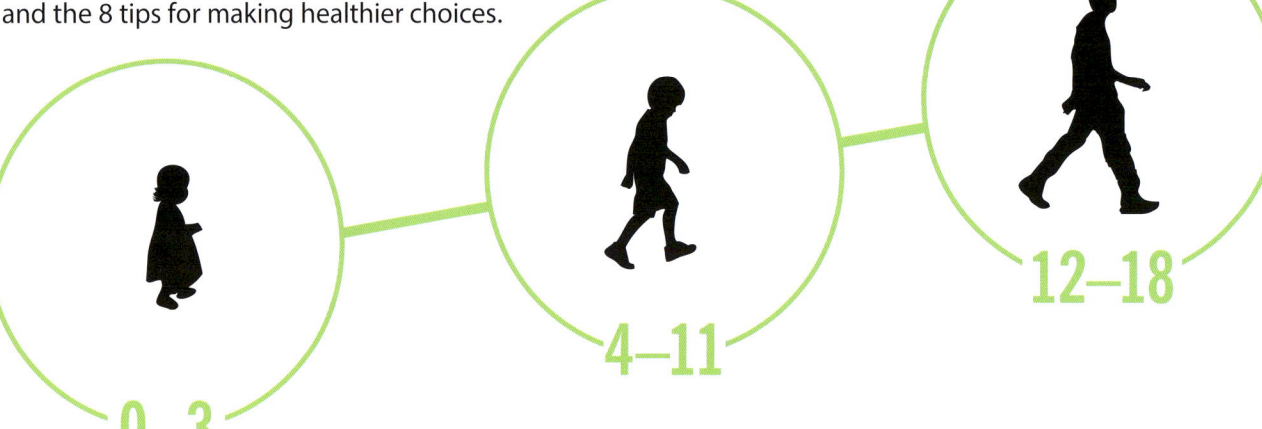

The human life cycle

Babies and toddlers (0–3 years)
- Babies grow a lot during this stage and their nutritional and energy needs are high.
- They usually drink breast or formula milk until they are 6 months old.
- Around 6 months, solid foods can be introduced to supply extra nutrients, such as iron (as the babies' own stores will be reduced) and carbohydrates (for energy).
- This gradual change from milk to solid foods is known as weaning.
- From 1 year, whole milk becomes an important nutrient source.
- This age group should not be given too much fibre because it can be difficult to digest. Also, if they feel 'full' they may miss out on other important nutrients.

Childhood (4–11 years)
- Children grow quickly during this stage and their nutritional and energy needs are very high.
- Children need protein to help their body grow.
- They need calcium to help build bones and teeth.
- Healthy eating habits should be encouraged at this stage and high sugar snacks avoided.

NUTRITION THROUGH LIFE

ACTIVITY...
Design a leaflet aimed at pregnant women. You might want to include information on:
- The nutrients that are important.
- The foods that should be avoided.

EXTENSION ACTIVITY...
Explain your choice of dish for your practical. You should include:
- A list of the main nutrients found in the ingredients.
- An explanation of how these nutrients meet the nutritional needs of your chosen life cycle stage.

PRACTICAL
Plan a suitable breakfast, lunch or dinner dish for 1 stage of the human life cycle.

19–64 **Pregnancy** **65+**

Adolescence (12–18 years)
- During puberty adolescents grow quickly and again their nutritional and energy needs are very high.
- They need protein for growth and repair.
- They need iron to prevent anaemia. This is particularly important in teenage girls because of the blood they lose during menstruation.

Adulthood (19–64 years)
- Nutritional requirements do not change greatly throughout this stage, so adults should try to maintain a healthy, balanced diet.
- As people age, their metabolism (the rate at which they burn energy) slows down. Adults should be careful not to consume more energy than they use or they will put on weight.

Pregnancy
- A healthy, balanced diet is important for pregnant or pre-conception women. They need a variety of nutrients to stay healthy and help their babies grow.
- They need folic acid for the growth of the foetus and to help prevent certain birth defects. This can be taken as a folic acid supplement.
- They should reduce their alcohol and caffeine intake.
- They should avoid certain foods, which can damage their unborn babies, such as raw and undercooked meat and eggs, foods high in vitamin A, unpasteurised dairy and certain soft cheeses.
- They do not need to 'eat for two' throughout pregnancy. Energy needs only increase in the last 3 months.

Old age (65+)
- Energy requirements generally decrease.
- A healthy, balanced diet is important to provide all the nutrients the body needs to stay healthy and fight off illness.

HEALTHY EATING

17. Vegetarianism

We are learning about:
- The different types of vegetarian diets
- The reasons why some people choose to become vegetarians
- Non-dairy sources of protein/meat alternatives

CORE COMPETENCE
By the age of 14 pupils should "…understand that people eat or avoid certain foods according to religion, culture, ethical belief or personal choices."

Today people choose to follow many different types of diet. Someone following a vegetarian diet chooses not to eat any meat, poultry, game, fish, shellfish or other animal products.

Types of vegetarian diets

There are many different types of vegetarian diets:

Lacto-ovo-vegetarians eat both dairy products and eggs. This is the most common type of vegetarian diet.

Lacto-vegetarians eat dairy products but avoid eggs.

Vegans do not eat dairy products, eggs, or any other products that are derived from animals.

Gelatine
Have you ever wondered what makes sweets chewy? It is an ingredient called gelatine, which is made from animal ligaments, tendons and bones. It is used in a lot of sweets, desserts and very low-fat products. It should be listed in the ingredients.

The reasons why some people choose to become vegetarians

Do you know anyone who is a vegetarian? Do you know the reasons why they became one? There are many different reasons why people choose to become vegetarians but one of the main reasons is that they believe it is cruel to kill animals and eat parts of their body. Here are some of the other reasons why people choose to become vegetarians:

- *Personal* – Some people simply do not like the taste of meat.
- *Religion* – Some religions do not permit their followers to eat meat.
- *Health* – Some people chose to become a vegetarian for health reasons because meat is high in saturated fat.
- *Environment* – Some people believe that meat production pollutes the environment more than crop production.
- *Social* – Some people are influenced by their friends and family. If their parents or siblings are vegetarians then they are more likely to become vegetarians too.
- *Economic* – Meat is more expensive than plant based foods.

FOR DISCUSSION…
Discuss a range of advantages and disadvantages of following a vegetarian diet.

The Vegetarian Society is a charity that exists to influence, inspire and support people to embrace and maintain a vegetarian lifestyle. It works constructively with businesses, government agencies, policy makers and professionals, whilst always remaining independent. The Vegetarian Society has produced its own trademark that appears on food and products which meet its strict criteria.

Source: https://www.vegsoc.org

VEGETARIANISM

Some food companies and retailers have designed their own logos to make it easy for consumers to recognise which foods are suitable for vegetarians. These logos usually include a capital 'V' on a green background.

RESEARCH ACTIVITY...
Use the Internet to research some famous or celebrity vegetarians. Try to discover the reasons behind their decision to become vegetarian.

Non-dairy sources of protein/meat alternatives

In Chapter 8 we learned that the Eatwell Guide contains a section called 'Beans, pulses, fish, eggs, meat and other proteins'. We are now going to learn about other sources of protein.

Food companies have developed a range of products that are considered meat substitutes or alternatives.

Textured vegetable protein (TVP)/textured soy protein

Quorn and Tofu are common examples of TVP foods that vegetarians often include in their diet instead of meat.

Nuts/pulses
Nuts and pulses are both examples of foods that are high in protein and therefore important in the diets of vegetarians.

ACTIVITY...
What nutrients might a vegetarian diet lack? Identify where a vegetarian could source these nutrients.

ACTIVITY...
Suggest some alternatives for the following common meat dishes:
- Chicken stir-fry
- Beef curry
- Beef burgers and chips

EXTENSION ACTIVITY...
Produce a report on meat alternatives suitable for vegetarians. You could include the following headings:
- Cost
- Texture
- Flavour
- Skill required
- Any other relevant factors

ACTIVITY...
CLASS DEBATE

Plan a class debate using one of the following motions or make up one of your own:
- 'Everyone should follow a vegetarian diet, it is healthier.'
- 'Vegetarians are more likely to become anaemic than meat eaters.'

You should have speakers for and against the statement and a chairperson to keep order.

PRACTICAL
Plan a dish using a meat alternative, such as Quorn or Tofu.

39

HEALTHY EATING

18. Food allergies and intolerances

We are learning about:
- What food allergies and intolerances are
- The symptoms of allergies and intolerances
- How to manage and treat allergies and intolerances

CORE COMPETENCE

By the age of 14 pupils should "…understand that people eat or avoid certain foods according to religion, culture, ethical belief or personal choices."

Pupils should also "…use nutrition and allergy information on food labels to help make informed food and drink choices."

Sometimes people's bodies react in an adverse way to certain foods. This can be caused by a food allergy or intolerance. It is important we learn about food allergies and intolerances so that we can recognise the symptoms and know how to manage or treat them. It will also help us plan meals for a wide range of dietary needs.

Food allergies

A food allergy is when the body's immune system has an adverse reaction to food. Food allergies are often mild but in some severe cases they can be life threatening.

Foods associated with allergies

- Eggs
- Milk
- Peanuts
- Fish
- Shellfish

The symptoms of allergies

- Swelling of the tongue
- Shortness of breath
- Itchy skin or rash
- Vomiting
- Dizziness

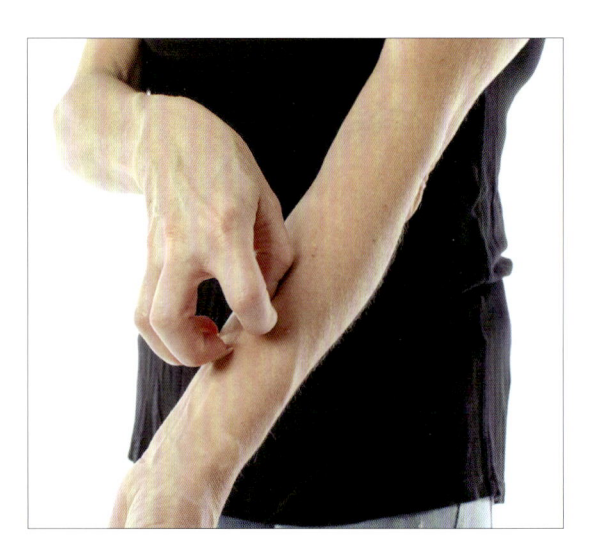

Most symptoms occur within two hours of digestion, however, sometimes a reaction may occur within minutes of eating.

Anaphylaxis – is a reaction that can happen to people with severe allergies. Anaphylactic shock is when a person with a severe allergy reacts to food. They may have several symptoms all at the same time, including difficulty breathing, vomiting, dizziness and a rapid heartbeat.

How to manage or treat allergies

- The best way to manage a food allergy is to avoid any food that causes a reaction.
- It is important to read food labels and ingredient lists carefully.
- Antihistamines can be used to treat mild to moderate allergic reactions.
- People who have been diagnosed with a severe food allergy should be treated with an injection of adrenaline as soon as they have a reaction. This injection is often referred to as an epi-pen.

FOOD ALLERGIES AND INTOLERANCES

Food intolerances

According to the NHS, around 1 or 2 people out of every 100 in the UK have a food allergy, but food intolerances are more common. Unlike a food allergy, the symptoms of a food intolerance may not occur straight after eating food, it could take several hours.

Types of food intolerances

Lactose intolerance – occurs when the body can't digest lactose, which is found in milk and dairy products.

Coeliac disease – occurs when the body reacts negatively to gluten. However, coeliac disease is not an allergy or intolerance to gluten, it is an autoimmune condition, which occurs when the immune system mistakes substances found inside gluten as a threat to the body and attacks them. Gluten is a protein found in wheat, rye and barley that damages the intestines of people with coeliac disease. Symptoms include diarrhoea, bloating and weight loss. Coeliac disease can be accurately diagnosed with a blood test and biopsy. About 1 in 100 people in the UK have coeliac disease, but it is estimated that around half a million have not been diagnosed.

Foods associated with intolerances

- Dairy products
- Wheat
- Gluten
- Yeast

The symptoms of intolerances

- Stomach pain
- Bloating
- Diarrhoea

How to manage intolerances

Like food allergies, the best way to manage a food intolerance is to avoid any food that causes a reaction.

ACTIVITY…

Design an information leaflet for teenagers about food allergies and intolerances. You might want to include:
- A definition for food allergy and food intolerance.
- The symptoms for each condition.
- The foods associated with each condition.
- How to manage and treat each condition.

ACTIVITY…

Imagine it is your birthday and you are planning a party for your friends. One of your friends is intolerant to wheat. Suggest 3 party food items that would be suitable for your friend to eat.

PRACTICAL

Plan 1 party food dish that would be suitable for a friend with a gluten intolerance.

HEALTHY EATING

19. Osteoporosis

We are learning about:
- What osteoporosis is
- The causes of osteoporosis
- How we can reduce our risk of developing osteoporosis

CORE COMPETENCE
By the age of 14 pupils should "…understand the implications of dietary excess or deficiency."

Osteoporosis is also known as 'brittle bone disease'. It is a condition that weakens the bones, making them more likely to break. It is important we learn about what causes osteoporosis so we can reduce our risk of developing it.

DID YOU KNOW?
- Osteoporosis affects around 3 million people in the UK.
- Every year more than 300,000 people receive hospital treatment for fragility fractures because of osteoporosis.

Source: Figures from The National Osteoporosis Society, https://www.nos.org.uk

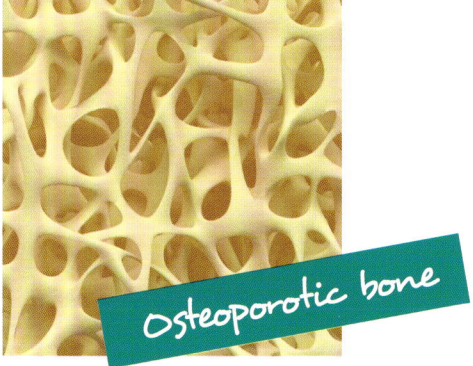

Healthy bone

Osteoporotic bone

The causes of osteoporosis

There are several factors that increase a person's risk of developing osteoporosis. Unfortunately, the more risk factors a person has, the greater their risk of developing osteoporosis is.

Some of the main factors that can increase a person's risk of developing osteoporosis are outlined below:

Diet – A diet low in calcium and vitamin D may increase the risk of developing osteoporosis.

Lifestyle – Smoking or a high alcohol intake may increase the risk of developing osteoporosis.

Gender – Women are more likely to develop osteoporosis than men.

Age – As we get older, the risk of developing osteoporosis increases.

Family history – Genetics may affect our bone health and therefore our risk of developing osteoporosis.

Body weight – People who are underweight or have a BMI of 19 or less have a greater risk of osteoporosis.

ACTIVITY…
Research 1 of the factors above in greater detail. For example:
- Why are women more likely to develop osteoporosis?
- How does age affect bone density?

Peak Bone Mass

Unfortunately, our bone density naturally decreases with age. This is why it is so important we look after our bones when we are young to achieve peak bone mass. Peak bone mass is when our bones are at their hardest/strongest. It is achieved in girls around the age of 18 and boys by the age of 20.

How can we reduce our risk of osteoporosis?

Include calcium and vitamin D in our diet – Calcium helps build healthy, strong bones and vitamin D helps our bodies to absorb calcium. For most of us, our vitamin D requirement comes from natural sunlight reacting with our skin.

Avoid smoking – Smoking inhibits the absorption of calcium.

OSTEOPOROSIS

Limit any alcohol intake – Alcohol affects the body's ability to absorb calcium effectively.

Take part in weight bearing activity – Weight bearing activity helps to improve our bone density and strength. For example, walking, jogging or aerobics.

Calcium content of foods

Food	Quantity	mg
Milk skimmed	100 ml	122
Milk semi-skimmed	100 ml	120
Milk whole	100 ml	118
Cheese (cheddar)	100 g	739
Sardines (in oil)	100 g	500
White bread	100 g	177

Source: Figures from 'Healthy Living for Strong Bones', a leaflet published by the National Osteoporosis Society

How much calcium do we need?

The Reference Nutrient Intake for 11–18 year boys is 1000 mg each day.

The Reference Nutrient Intake for 11–18 year old girls is 800 mg each day.

PRACTICAL

MI SM TPD BC

Plan a healthy recipe that is high in calcium. For example, cheesecake or macaroni cheese.

43

HEALTHY EATING

20. Iron deficiency anaemia

We are learning about:
- What iron deficiency anaemia is
- The causes of iron deficiency anaemia
- The symptoms of iron deficiency anaemia

CORE COMPETENCE
By the age of 14 pupils should "…understand the implications of dietary excess or deficiency."

It is important we learn about what happens to our body when we do not achieve the amount of nutrients we need. If we understand the causes of diet related disorders then we can take greater responsibility for our own health and well-being.

The causes of iron deficiency anaemia
Anaemia is caused by a deficiency of the mineral iron. We need iron to produce red blood cells, so a lack of iron in our diet reduces the amount of red blood cells in our bodies. Our bodies need these red blood cells to store and transport oxygen.

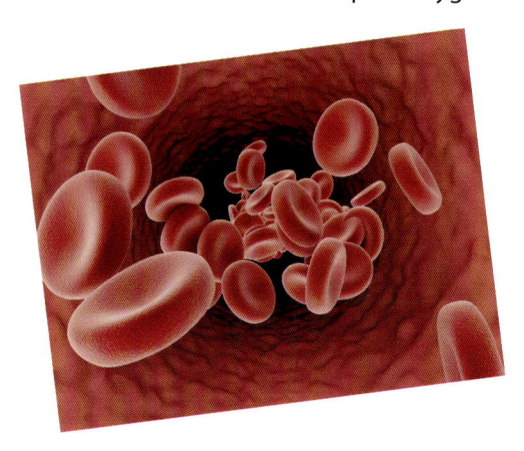

The symptoms of iron deficiency anaemia
- Tiredness
- Difficulty concentrating
- Pale skin
- Palpitations

The sources of iron
- Green leafy vegetables
- Red meat
- Shellfish
- Eggs
- Beans and lentils
- Dried fruit
- Fortified cereal

DID YOU KNOW?
Vitamin C helps our bodies absorb iron. There are two types of iron.
- *Haem* – easily absorbed by the body.
- *Non-haem* – not as easily absorbed by the body.

When we eat foods high in vitamin C it helps our body absorb non-haem iron.

DID YOU KNOW?
- Teenage girls or women who have heavy periods are at greater risk of developing iron deficiency anaemia. This is because they may not consume enough iron to replace the iron that they lose through their blood during menstruation.
- Iron deficiency anaemia is common in pregnant women. This is because the foetus takes the iron it needs from the mother.

IRON DEFICIENCY ANAEMIA

RESEARCH ACTIVITY...
MI | SM | TPD | ICT

Research the different types of supplements for iron.

ACTIVITY...
MI | SM | TPD | ICT | COM

Investigate the role of supplements as a source of iron.
- Consider the advantages and disadvantages of taking supplements.
- Comment on your findings and conclude with your personal opinion on supplements as a source of iron.

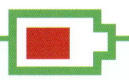

PRACTICAL
MI | SM | TPD | BC

Plan a beef and vegetable stir-fry.

ACTIVITY...
MI | SM | TPD | BC

- Read the conversation opposite between 14 year old Gemma and an online counsellor.
- Imagine you are the counsellor and write a reply to Gemma, advising her on what she could do to help improve her symptoms.

Insta-chat...

Online Counsellor
Teen helpline. How can I help?

Gemma
I'm writing to you because I don't know who else to talk to. Nobody understands. I'm tired all the time even though I love sleeping! Things haven't been going well for me in school. I just got my report and my teachers have said that my grades should be higher. Some teachers said that I find it difficult to concentrate in class. I guess they are right! My PE teacher shouted at me the other day because apparently I wasn't putting enough energy into our activity! She didn't understand that I actually felt really weak that morning.

My parents are also giving me a hard time. They say I'm not eating properly now that I've become a vegetarian. I became a vegetarian in Year 10. Lots of my friends are too and their parents don't have a problem with it!

What should I do? I hope you can help.

Thanks so much, Gemma

Online Counsellor
Typing...

45

HEALTHY EATING

21. Obesity

We are learning about:
- What obesity is
- Body Mass Index (BMI)
- The effects of obesity
- How to avoid obesity

> **CORE COMPETENCE**
> By the age of 14 pupils should "…understand the importance of energy balance and the implications of dietary excess or deficiency."

A person who is obese is very overweight. The rates of obesity in Northern Ireland and around the world have increased significantly in recent years. In this section we are going to learn why obesity is increasing, the impact it can have on our health and how we can avoid it.

Body Mass Index (BMI)

The BMI score is used as a measure of how healthy an adult's weight is based on his or her height. It can also be used to determine if a person is obese.

> **Note:** The chart below is designed for adults. It is not suitable for anyone under 18 years old.

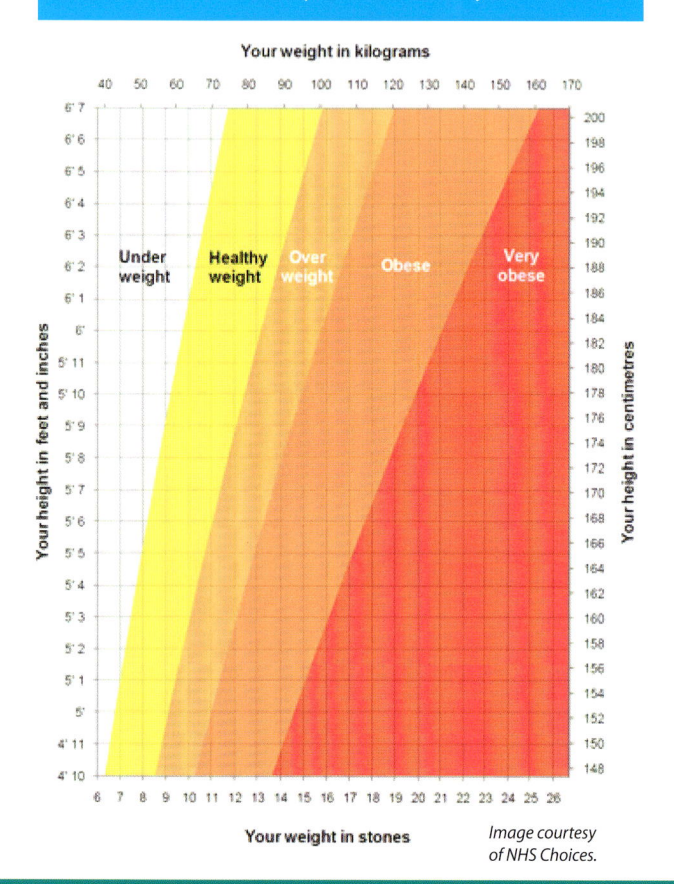

Image courtesy of NHS Choices.

The BMI for an adult can also be calculated by using this formula:

$$BMI = \frac{Weight\ (kg)}{Height^2\ (m)}$$

For most adults:
- a BMI of 25 to 29.9 is considered overweight.
- a BMI of 30 to 39.9 is considered obese.
- a BMI of 40 or above is considered severely obese.

> **THINK ABOUT…**
> What type of person could have a high BMI but very little body fat? Does this still mean that this person is overweight?

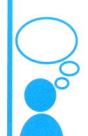

The Health Survey Northern Ireland (2014) reported that 18% of children between 2 and 10 years old were overweight and 7% were obese. That's 25% of children classed as overweight or obese. The survey also revealed that 37% of adults in Northern Ireland were classified as overweight and an additional 24% were classified as obese.

Source: Figures from 'Health Survey Northern Ireland: First Results 2013/14', http://www.dhsspsni.gov.uk/

OBESITY

THINK ABOUT...
Why do you think the rates of obesity have increased in recent years?

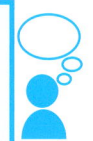

Energy Balance
When our 'energy balance' is even, our energy input and energy output are equal. This is important, as when we 'burn off' (use) all the calories that we consume, our weight is likely to remain the same. However, if we consume more calories than we can 'burn off' then we are likely to put on weight.

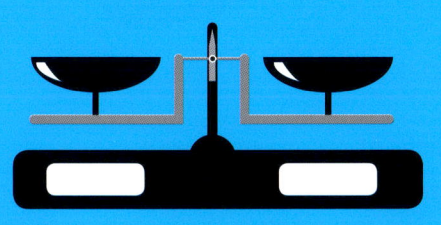

ACTIVITY...
Record your energy input and output for yesterday. Write down:
- your energy input – all the foods and drinks you consumed.
- your energy output – anything physically active you did. This doesn't just mean PE or team games, walking to school and helping with the housework counts too!

Do you think your energy input and output were fairly equal yesterday? If not, how could you make your energy balance more even?

The effects of obesity
Being overweight or obese can affect the following:
- *Health* – Obesity can increase the chances of people developing conditions such as cancer, diabetes or heart disease.
- *Mobility* – Obesity can cause mobility issues and make it difficult for people to move around comfortably.
- *Self esteem* – Sometimes obesity can cause low self esteem, as people become unhappy with their body image.

How to avoid obesity
Here are some ways to help us avoid obesity:
- *Follow a healthy diet* – Use the Eatwell Guide and 8 tips as a starting point. Also try to include foods that are high in fibre, as these keep us fuller for longer and discourage snacking.
- *Keep our energy balance even* – If our energy input and output are equal, we are less likely to put on weight.
- *Portion control* – We need to be aware of how much food we are eating (our energy input). If we stick to appropriate portion sizes for each meal, we are less likely to put on weight.
- *Exercise more* – Exercise 'burns' calories and increases our energy output. If we burn off as many calories as we consume (energy input), we are less likely to put on weight.

EXTENSION ACTIVITY...
HEALTH AND FITNESS LOG

Keep a log of your diet and exercise for 1 week. Reflect on your log and see if you can think of any improvements you could make to your health and fitness routine.

47

HEALTHY EATING

22. Coronary heart disease

We are learning about:
- What coronary heart disease is
- The causes of coronary heart disease
- The effects of coronary heart disease
- How to avoid coronary heart disease

> **CORE COMPETENCE**
> By the age of 14 pupils should "…understand the importance of energy balance and the implications of dietary excess or deficiency."

Although it is only the size of a human fist, our heart is one of the most important organs in our body. We need it to pump blood around our body so it is important we learn how to look after it and keep it healthy.

Coronary heart disease occurs when our coronary arteries become narrow because of a build up of fatty material or plaque. This reduces the blood flowing to the heart, forcing it to pump harder. The images below show the difference between healthy and unhealthy arteries.

A healthy artery where the blood flows through normally.

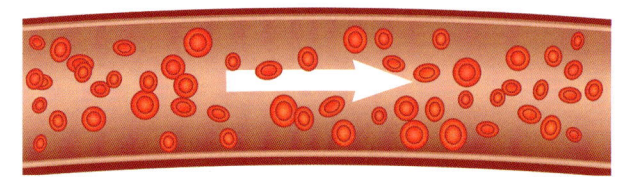

A partly blocked artery where the blood flow is restricted.

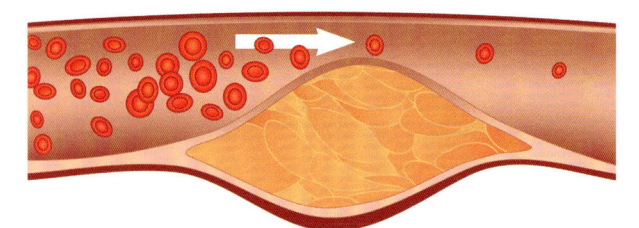

A significantly blocked artery where it is very difficult for blood to pass through.

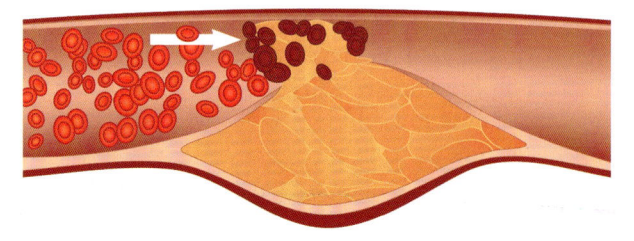

DID YOU KNOW?

Our heart beats around 70 times in just one minute.

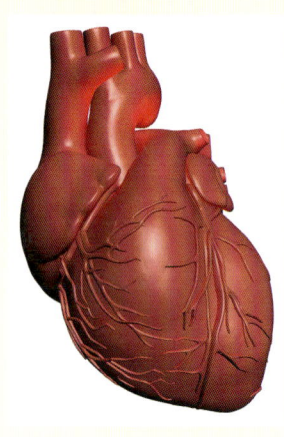

The causes of coronary heart disease

There are many causes of coronary heart disease. Some of the main factors that are thought to increase a person's risk of developing coronary heart disease are outlined below:

- *Smoking* – Smoking damages the lining of our arteries. According to the British Heart Foundation, smokers are almost twice as likely to have a heart attack as people who have never smoked.

- *High blood cholesterol* – Increased cholesterol in the blood clogs up the arteries with fatty material or plaque.

- *High blood pressure* – (also known as 'hypertension') puts strain on the heart.

- *Being overweight* – Research suggests that being overweight or obese can increase blood pressure and raise blood cholesterol levels.

CORONARY HEART DISEASE

- *Family history* – Unfortunately coronary heart disease can be hereditary and the risk can be greater if a family member has suffered from the condition.
- *Gender* – Males are at greater risk of developing coronary heart disease than females.
- *Age* – The older a person is then the greater their risk of developing coronary heart disease.

Unfortunately, the more risk factors a person has the greater their risk of developing coronary heart disease.

The effects of coronary heart disease

If our arteries become very blocked then it is difficult for our blood to pump around the body and for blood to flow properly. This can result in a heart attack.

DID YOU KNOW?

According to the National Health Service, coronary heart disease is responsible for around 73,000 deaths in the UK each year, with about 1 in 6 men and 1 in 10 women dying from the disease.

How to avoid coronary heart disease

- Reduce the amount of saturated fat in the diet
- Reduce the amount of salt in the diet
- Avoid smoking
- Exercise regularly
- Minimise stress

RESEARCH ACTIVITY...

- Research what other risk factors are associated with coronary heart disease.
- Make notes on your findings, using the headings: diet, lifestyle and other.

PRACTICAL

Prepare a healthy dish that is suitable for someone with coronary heart disease. It should be low in salt, low in saturated fat and (if possible) high in fibre.

23. Factors affecting our food choice

We are learning about:
- The factors that affect our food choice
- Planning meals for a diverse range of people

CORE COMPETENCE
By the age of 14 pupils should "...Understand that people eat or avoid certain foods according to religion, culture, ethical belief, or personal choices."

We all have our own personal likes and dislikes when it comes to food but there are many other factors that affect food choices. It is important we learn about these different factors, as it helps us to understand more about each other.

ACTIVITY...
- List your top 10 favourite foods.
- List 2 foods that you do not like.
- List 2 foods that you have never tried before.

THINK ABOUT...
Why do you choose the foods you eat?

Preferences
Generally people will eat foods they like the taste of and avoid those they don't (or think they don't) like.

Health
Some people choose to avoid certain foods for health reasons. For example, people suffering from coronary heart disease may decide to reduce the amount of saturated fat in their diet.

Allergies and intolerances
Some people's bodies react in an adverse way to certain foods, so they tend to avoid these foods.

Individual energy and nutrient needs
People's nutritional requirements change throughout life. For example, children need more calcium than adults, as they are still building their bones and teeth, and may choose to eat foods with

HEALTHY EATING

a higher calcium content. Energy needs are also very different from person to person, for example, active people have a higher energy output than people who are less active so may choose higher energy foods (higher energy input).

Cost
Some people choose to spend more on food than others. For example, they may choose a chicken dish instead of steak in a restaurant as it is less expensive.

Environmental and ethical concerns
People with specific environmental or ethical concerns may choose different foods to those without these concerns. For example, many vegetarians choose not to eat meat, as they believe it is cruel to kill animals to eat, and people who are concerned with the environment are more likely to choose organic foods.

Religious beliefs
People's religious beliefs may affect their choice of foods. Some religions do not allow their members to eat certain animals, others can only eat animals slaughtered in a particular way and some cannot eat any meat at all. According to the British Nutrition Foundation, the following religions require the food rules in the table below.

Halal foods – are the foods that Muslims are allowed to eat or drink according to Islamic law.

Kosher foods – are foods that conform to Jewish law. Food that is not kosher is commonly referred to as **treif**.

ACTIVITY...
Research 1 of the following types of food:
- Halal
- Kosher

ACTIVITY...
Imagine you have to plan an event for a wide range of people, including some from the following religious backgrounds:
- Islam
- Judaism
- Buddhism

Design a menu that will cater for the needs of all your guests.

EXTENSION ACTIVITY...
Justify your menu choice, explaining how it caters for the needs of all your guests.

PRACTICAL
Plan a dish suitable for a religion of your choice.

Religion	Meats they can and can't eat				
	Pork	Beef	Lamb	Chicken	Fish
Islam	✗	Halal only	Halal only	Halal only	✓
Hinduism	✗	✗	✓	✓	✓
Judaism	✗	Kosher only	Kosher only	Kosher only	✓
Sikhism	✗	✗	✓	✓	✓
Buddhism (strict)	✗	✗	✗	✗	✗
Seventh-day Adventist Church	✗	✗	✗	✓	✓
Rastafari Movement	✗	✗	✗	✗	✗

Source: Food A Fact of Life, http://www.foodafactoflife.org.uk, courtesy of the British Nutrition Foundation

FOOD AROUND THE WORLD

24. Food around the world

We are learning about:
- A range of foods from around the world
- How culture can affect our food choice
- Globalisation

CORE COMPETENCE
By the age of 14 pupils should…"understand that people eat or avoid certain foods according to religion, culture, ethical belief, or personal choices."

Today there is such a wide range of foods available to us. In our local supermarket we can buy foods grown all over the world, including oranges from Spain, coffee from Brazil and rice from India. These foods are imported from other countries, often because they don't grow well in our climate and need:

- higher temperatures
- more sunshine
- less rainfall
- different soil types

EXTENSION ACTIVITY…
- Keep a food diary for a day.
- Record where each food you eat comes from.
- You might need to look up 'the country of origin' on the label.

How culture influences our food choices
Most countries have their own traditional foods, some of which are shown below. They also have their own ways of preparing and eating food, for example:

- In England, many people enjoy drinking tea with biscuits in the afternoon.
- In Italy, many people buy fresh ingredients on a daily basis to prepare their meals.
- In India, food is often prepared in a special oven called a tandoor.

America
India
Mexico
Spain
England
Japan

ACTIVITY…
- Which of these world foods is the healthiest?
- Give reasons for your answer.

HEALTHY EATING

When people move from one country to live in another they will bring some of these traditions with them. This is why many of the dishes available to us locally are influenced by other cultures, such as Chinese dishes cooked in the local takeaway.

THINK ABOUT... *TPD*
- What is your favourite dish?
- Where does it come from?

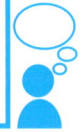

Globalisation

All of these food choices have been made available to us because of globalisation, the process of the world becoming more interconnected. In the past it was both slow and difficult to transport products and people. Today, modern transport (eg planes) and communication (eg Internet) links allow us to connect more effectively with people around the world.

RESEARCH ACTIVITY... *TPD MI BC*

Research the traditional foods of 1 country of your choice.

Present your research to the class as a PowerPoint. Include the following information:
- A world map showing the location of the country.
- The country's culture and how it has influenced traditional food.
- Photographs of the country's most popular foods.

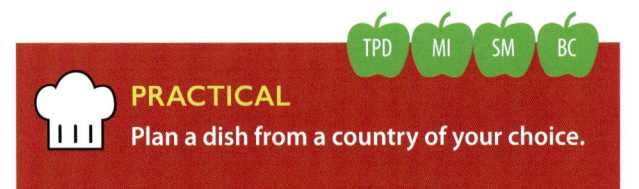

PRACTICAL *TPD MI SM BC*
Plan a dish from a country of your choice.

25. Labelling

We are learning about:
- The importance of food labels
- Mandatory information
- Voluntary information

CORE COMPETENCE
By the age of 14 pupils should "...use nutrition and allergy information on food labels to help make informed food and drink choices."

The importance of food labels

Have you ever thought about how difficult food shopping would be if the products were unlabelled? How would we know what is in the food? It is important that we learn about labelling so that we can make informed choices and take greater responsibility for our own health.

Who controls this aspect of food safety?

There is special legislation that relates to the labelling of food. In Northern Ireland, food labelling is controlled by the Food Information Regulations (Northern Ireland) 2014.

This legislation covers:
- What information needs to go on a label.
- The mandatory and voluntary information.

The Environmental Health Officer has the responsibility of enforcing these regulations and making sure that information on a food label is accurate and not misleading.

LABELLING

Mandatory information (must be on the label)
1. The name of the food
2. List of ingredients
3. Food allergens and intolerances
4. The quantity of certain ingredients
5. Net quantity
6. Indication of minimum durability ('use by' or 'best before' dates)
7. Storage conditions and/or conditions of use
8. Name or business name and address of the food business operator
9. Place of origin or provenance of food (if required)
10. Instructions of use (if needed)
11. Alcohol strength
12. Nutrition information

List of ingredients

Ingredients:
Wheat, Flour, Water, Vegetable Oil (Rapeseed Oil), Beef (13%), Beef Kidney (10%), Onion, Cornflour, Salt, Dextrose, Yeast Extract, Malted **Barley** Extract, **Milk** Proteins, Black Pepper, Onion Powder, Glucose Syrup.

Food allergens
Allergens such as peanuts, wheat, milk, eggs, shellfish and many others must be **highlighted** within the ingredients list, as shown in the list of ingredients above. If there is no list of ingredients then there must be a statement on the packaging, such as 'contains peanuts'.

The change to allergen labelling rules in 2014 removed allergy advice boxes but these can be replaced with a statement such as 'Food allergens are highlighted in the ingredients list'.

Nutrition information
It is important we know what is inside the food we eat. The nutritional label helps us identify the nutrients in our food, such as fats, carbohydrates and protein. It is a useful source of information for consumers to use.

Nutrition labelling is mandatory if a nutrition claim or health claim is made. From December 2016 nutrition labelling will become a mandatory requirement.

DID YOU KNOW?

Do you know why ingredients are listed in a particular order?

They are listed in 'descending order of weight'. This means that the heaviest ingredients are listed first.

THINK ABOUT…

Why is it important that any allergens are highlighted on food labels?

Voluntary information (front of pack labelling)
In recent years, food companies have developed their own front of pack labelling, so labels varied from product to product. With the new legislation, all front of pack labelling in the UK will look the same. This should make it less confusing for consumers and help them to make healthier food choices.

The coloured shading in the label (below left) tells us if a food contains low (green), medium (amber) or high (red) levels of fat, sugar and salt. The table (below right) explains this colour coding, showing the nutritional information for 100 g of food.

Each pack contains
Energy 2267 kJ / 542kcal (27%), Fat 20g (28%), Saturates 6.4g (32%), Sugars 7.6g (8%), Salt 2.4g (42%)
of your reference intake
Typical values per 100g: Energy 756kJ / 213kcal

Source: 'Guide to creating a front of pack (FoP) nutrition label for pre-packed products sold through retail outlets'. Contains public sector information licensed under the Open Government Licence v3.0.

Text	LOW	MEDIUM	HIGH	
Colour code	Green	Amber	Red	
Fat	≤ 3.0g/100g	> 3.0g to ≤ 17.5g/100g	> 17.5g/100g	> 21g/portion
Saturates	≤ 1.5g/100g	> 1.5g to ≤ 5.0g/100g	> 5.0g/100g	> 6.0g/portion
(Total) Sugars	≤ 5.0g/100g	> 5.0g and ≤ 22.5g /100g	> 22.5g/100g	> 27g/portion
Salt	≤ 0.3g/100g	> 0.3g to ≤ 1.5g/100g	>1.5g/100g	>1.8g/portion

Note: portion size criteria apply to portions/serving sizes greater than 100 g.

HEALTHY EATING

ACTIVITY...
- Select a food label of your choice and stick it onto a file page or into your workbook.
- Identify all the mandatory information (the 12 things that must be shown) on your chosen label.

ACTIVITY...
Look at the nutrition label on a food item.

Use the colour coding table on the previous page to work out if the fat, sugar and salt content is:

a) red

b) amber

c) green

THINK ABOUT...
How could we improve food labels to make it easier for consumers to make healthier food choices?

EXTENSION ACTIVITY...
Design your own food label for a food product of your choice (eg, a sandwich).

HOME ECONOMICS
INDEPENDENT LIVING

INDEPENDENT LIVING

26. Consumerism

We are learning about:
- What a consumer is
- Examples of products and services
- Types of purchases

We are all consumers. A consumer is a person who buys products or uses services.

> **THINK ABOUT...** TPD
> What do you think it means when people say "we live in a consumer driven society"?

Examples of products
- Mobile phones
- Sports equipment
- Computer games
- Groceries
- Makeup
- Clothes

Examples of services
- Hairdressing
- Football coaching
- Music lessons
- Cinema
- Public transport

> **ACTIVITY...** TPD SM
> - List 5 products or services you have bought or used recently.
> - Choose 1 product or service and explain what influenced your decision to purchase it.

Types of purchases

There are two main types of purchases we make as consumers:

Planned purchases
Most of the time we plan our purchases, thinking about or even researching a product or service before buying it. Expensive items are often planned purchases, as most people have to save up money to buy them. For example, most people couldn't afford to buy a new mobile phone every week, month or even every year. They will often research the phone they want before purchasing it, as they will be using it for some time.

Impulse purchases
Sometimes we spontaneously buy products or use services, without planning to purchase them. Inexpensive items are often impulse purchases, needing less thought or research than expensive items, as people rarely need to save up money for them. For example, have you ever gone into a shop for something in particular but left the shop with other items as well, such as a magazine, drink or chocolate bar? These are all impulse purchases.

> **ACTIVITY...** TPD BC
> - List 2 products you regularly purchase on impulse.
> - What influences you to buy these items?

> **EXTENSION ACTIVITY...** MI TPD SM
> Sean is planning to buy a new mobile phone.
> - List 5 things Sean might want to find out about before he decides on a new phone.
> - Where will he find this information?

56

27. Responsible Consumers

We are learning about:
- Consumer rights
- Consumer responsibilities
- Ethical consumers

It is important we learn about our consumer rights and responsibilities to become more effective as consumers.

Consumer rights

All consumers have the right to:

- *Information* – To have access to the information needed to make informed decisions.
- *A choice* – To have access to a range of suitable products and services to choose from.
- *Redress* – To receive a fair settlement for just claims (eg compensation for misrepresentation or unsatisfactory services).
- *An education* – To gain the knowledge and skills needed to make informed and confident choices.
- *A healthy and sustainable environment* – To live and work in a non-threatening environment that is sustainable for the well-being of present and future generations.

Consumer responsibilities

All consumers have the responsibility to:

- Keep informed
- Consider the consequences of their decisions
- Take responsibility for their decisions

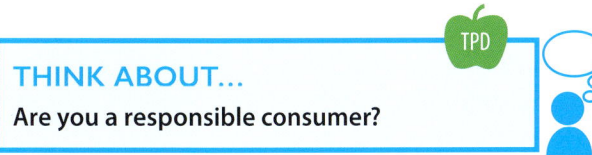

> **THINK ABOUT…**
> Are you a responsible consumer?

Ethical consumers

Ethical consumers purchase goods and services that are produced in a way that does not harm or exploit the environment, animals or people.

Ethical products and services

- *Organic foods* – This food is produced using environmentally and animal friendly farming methods. You will learn more about this in Chapter 29.
- *Local produce* – This is food that is grown, cooked, baked or produced in the local area. This food doesn't need to travel far from its source to where it is sold, which keeps the environmental impact of its journey low. The sale of local produce also benefits local farmers, who may be struggling to compete with supermarket prices. 
- *Fairtrade goods* – These goods are approved by the Fairtrade Foundation, which works to ensure better prices, working conditions and terms of trade for the farmers and workers that produce Fairtrade products. You will learn more about this in Chapter 29.
- *Recycled goods* – These are goods that are made from waste material. Recycled goods reduce the amount of waste that needs disposed of and also the amount of fresh materials needed to produce new goods.
- *Cruelty-free cosmetics and cleaning products* – These are products that have not been tested on animals.

INDEPENDENT LIVING

THINK ABOUT…
What ethical issues are important to you? How could you become a more ethical consumer?

RESEARCH ACTIVITY…
FOOD MILES

Food miles are the distance the food has travelled from its source to where it is sold.

Investigate the food miles of 3 different food products.

Find out the following information for each:
- The country of origin
- The food miles travelled

The food miles website will help you: http://www.foodmiles.com

RESEARCH ACTIVITY…
THE 3 RS

Working in a group, research the 3 Rs of recycling:
- Reduce
- Reuse
- Recycle

EXTENSION ACTIVITY…
Using your research on the 3 Rs, think of all the ways that your Home Economics class could reduce, reuse and recycle.

Plan a presentation to deliver this information to your class.

28. Factors that influence consumers

We are learning about:
- The factors that influence consumers

CORE COMPETENCE
By the age of 14 pupils should "Be aware that food choice depends on many personal and lifestyle factors."

As consumers we are influenced by many different factors. Some factors affect us more than others depending on our age, our lifestyle, our needs and wants, our education and experience, and how much money we have available to spend.

Personal
We all have our own personal likes and dislikes. This is what makes us unique. For example, you may choose a different perfume or aftershave from your friend because of the type of fragrance you like.

Cultural
Our cultural background can influence our choice of food, clothes and other purchasing decisions. For example, a girl might wear a long prom dress to her school formal but another girl from the Indian community might choose to wear a decorative sari instead.

FACTORS THAT INFLUENCE CONSUMERS

Ethical
Our ethical concerns can influence our purchases. For example, if you are an ethical consumer you are more likely to choose products that are local, Fairtrade or organic. We will learn more about this in Chapter 29.

Economic
The amount of money we have available to spend can influence the products and services we purchase. For example, you might want the latest computer game, pair of shoes or concert ticket but if you don't have the money to spend, you can't make these purchases.

Physiological
Physiological factors relate to our bodies and how they function. Their affect on our bodies can influence our purchases. For example, if you have a nut allergy you will be careful to choose food products that haven't been in contact with nuts.

Psychological
Psychological factors relate to our thoughts and feelings. They may influence our purchases because of how they affect our emotions. For example, many people will only choose branded food products because of an emotional association with particular products, even if they taste similar to the supermarket own-brand versions!

Social
We are often influenced by the people around us and care about the opinions of our families and friends. For example, you may decide to buy a particular pair of shoes because all your friends wear them.

ACTIVITY…

Read the case studies below.
- What factors do you think affected Andrew's choice of pizza? Give reasons to support your answer.
- List 3 products that you think Catherine would buy. What factors would influence Catherine's product choices the most? Give reasons to support your answer.

CASE STUDY 1

Andrew is 19 and has recently left home to study at university in Newcastle. He is having a party and has purchased some supermarket own-brand pizza to share with his friends.

CASE STUDY 2

Catherine is a vegetarian. She is very health conscious and likes to buy local produce. She has recently been diagnosed with coeliac disease.

ACTIVITY…

List 5 factors that influence your general product choices.

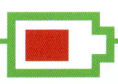

ACTIVITY…

- Think of 2 products or services that you purchased recently.
- For each purchase, explain in detail what factors affected your decision. For example, if you bought a pair of jeans because your friends also wear them it would mean you were influenced by social factors.

INDEPENDENT LIVING

29. Different types of food production

We are learning about:
- How to make responsible decisions as consumers
- Natural and processed foods
- The difference between conventional and organic farming
- Fairtrade products

CORE COMPETENCE
By the age of 14 pupils should… "Know that food is sold in different ways eg conventional and organic farming, fairtrade."

With so many food products available to us it is important we learn how our food is produced so that we can make informed and responsible choices about what we eat.

Natural foods
According to the Food Standards Agency, natural foods are comprised of ingredients "produced by nature, not the work of man or interfered with by man". Essentially this means that natural foods are minimally processed and do not contain any artificial additives.

Processed foods
Often people associate processed foods with being unhealthy, containing additives and having a low nutritional value. However, 'processed' covers a much broader range of foods. Most foods are processed in some form. Sometimes this is for convenience, such as to reduce preparation time, but often it is for food safety, such as the pasteurisation of dairy products to remove bacteria.

THINK ABOUT…
What natural and processed foods have you eaten recently? Write down 2 of each.

Organic farming
Organic food is produced using environmentally and animal friendly farming methods. For farming to be called organic it must:

- not use artificial chemical fertilisers.
- not use GM (genetically modified) crops or ingredients.
- restrict the use of pesticides.
- respect animal welfare.
- guarantee a free range lifestyle for farm animals.
- raise a diversity of crops and animals to rotate round the farm over several seasons.
- not use drugs, antibiotics or wormers routinely. Preventative methods should be used instead.

Soil Association
The Soil Association is a charity that campaigns for healthy, humane and sustainable food, farming and land use. An important part of their work involves certifying foods as 'organic'. The Soil Association Certification is the UK's largest organic certification body, responsible for certifying over 70% of all organic products sold in the country.

DID YOU KNOW?
According to the Soil Association's 2015 Organic Market Report, sales of organic products increased by 4% in 2014 to £1.86 billion. This increase was significant for a year when food prices fell by 1.9% and consumer spending by 1.1%.

Source: Figures from the Soil Association's 2015 Organic Market Report, http://www.soilassociation.org

DIFFERENT TYPES OF FOOD PRODUCTION

THINK ABOUT...
Why do you think the sales of organic foods have increased in recent years?

RESEARCH ACTIVITY...
Choose 1 of the 4 items below:
- 2 chicken breast fillets
- 2 litres of milk
- 6 eggs
- A bunch of bananas

Research the price of the regular and organic versions of the item.

Calculate the difference in price.

FOR DISCUSSION...
Discuss the reasons for the difference in price between the regular and organic versions of the items above.

Conventional farming
Unlike organic farming, conventional farming uses chemical fertilisers and pesticides to manage weeds and pests. It may also use drugs, antibiotics and wormers, GM crops and ingredients, and does not have to guarantee a free range lifestyle for animals.

ACTIVITY...
Watch 'The organic debate' video on Youtube to help you understand more about this topic:
https://www.youtube.com/watch?v=JWqq0Zga2AE

RESEARCH ACTIVITY...
Working in a group, research the advantages and disadvantages of:
 a) organic farming and
 b) conventional farming

You might find it helpful to look at the following areas:
- Costs
- Health
- Ethics
- Environment

Compare your findings on the 2 types of farming.

Fairtrade
Many of the food products we enjoy, such as bananas, sugar, rice, tea and coffee, are grown outside of the UK in developing countries. Many of the farmers who grow these foods have small farms, so the processing and sale of these products may be carried out by large companies. Some companies pay the farmers very little for their hard work so they can lower the prices of the finished products.

The Fairtrade Foundation works to ensure better prices, working conditions and terms of trade for these farmers and their workers. It also supports the development of these farmer and worker communities to give them more control over their futures and to protect the environment in which they live and work.

® The FAIRTRADE Mark means that the Fairtrade ingredients in the product have been produced by small-scale farmer organisations or plantations that meet Fairtrade social, economic and environmental standards.

PRACTICAL
Plan a recipe for muffins using Fairtrade bananas.

61

INDEPENDENT LIVING

30. Shopping Options

We are learning about:
- A range of shopping options available to consumers
- The advantages and disadvantages of different shopping options

Most of us like to visit different shops for clothes, food, electronic equipment and beauty products, and we all have our personal favourites. We are fortunate to have a wide range of shopping options to choose from. It is important we learn about the advantages and disadvantages of different shopping options so that we can choose the most suitable option for us.

Shopping options available to consumers

Shopping option	Advantages	Disadvantages
Local independent shop	• Personal service • Close to home	• Often more expensive • Stock may be limited
Supermarket	• A wide range of products available • Special offers and price promotions	• Impersonal service • May overspend and make impulse purchases
Market stall	• Range of local produce • Often cheaper prices	• Only available on certain days • May not have access to the range of products available from other shopping options
Specialist shop	• High quality products • Expert advice available	• Often more expensive • A limited range of products
Online shopping	• Available 24 hours a day, 7 days a week • A wide range of products available • Can purchase from the comfort of your own home	• Security issues (eg Internet or payment card fraud) • Don't get to handle the product before purchasing it • Have to pay postage costs • Don't get the product immediately
Shopping channels	• Unique products that may not be available to purchase on the high street • Can purchase from the comfort of your own home	• Don't get to handle the product before purchasing it • Time consuming • Don't get the product immediately

SHOPPING OPTIONS

THINK ABOUT... (TPD)
What other shopping options are available for people to choose from?

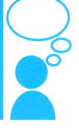

ACTIVITY... (MI, TPD, SM)
Read the case studies below and recommend the best shopping option for the following people. Give reasons for your answer.

CASE STUDY 1
Fiona is a student and is on a limited budget. She needs to buy some basic essentials such as bread and milk.

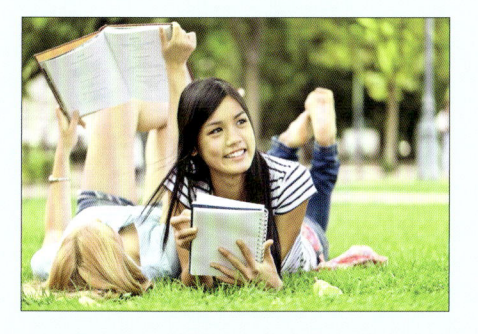

CASE STUDY 2
Maria and Patrick are married with children. Both parents work long hours and find shopping stressful.

CASE STUDY 3
Josie is nearly 78 years old. She finds it difficult to walk and depends on her walking frame to get around.

RESEARCH ACTIVITY... (MI, TPD, SM, MA)
Consumer investigator

Choose 2 shopping options to investigate.

Find out the prices of the following basic items within your 2 shopping options:

- 1 loaf of white bread
- 2 litres of milk
- 1 kg granulated sugar
- 250 g butter
- 160 teabags

Record your results in a table and create a bar chart to show your findings.

EXTENSION ACTIVITY... (MI, TPD, SM)
Using the same 2 shopping options as above, investigate 1 of the following facilities or services:

- Parking facilities
- Disability access
- Customer service
- Opening hours
- Variety of products
- Hygiene standards

For each option, rate the quality of the facility/service from 1–10 (with 10 being the highest).

Recommend how each shopping option could improve their facility/service.

INDEPENDENT LIVING

31. Online Shopping

We are learning about:
- Growth in online shopping
- Advantages and disadvantages of online shopping
- How to stay safe online

Growth in online shopping

Online shopping is a convenient method of shopping for many consumers. It has grown in popularity over recent years, particularly since mobile technology has made it even more accessible to the consumer. The table below shows the recent growth in online shopping sales for 2014 and 2015 in Europe.

Online retail sales	Online sales (£bn) 2014	Growth 2014	Online sales (£bn) 2015	Growth 2015
UK	£44.97	15.8%	£52.25	16.2%
Germany	£36.23	25.0%	£44.61	23.1%
France	£26.38	16.5%	£30.87	17.0%
Spain	£6.87	19.6%	£8.15	18.6%
Italy	£5.33	19.0%	£6.35	19.0%
Netherlands	£5.09	13.5%	£5.94	16.8%
Sweden	£3.61	15.5%	£4.17	15.5%
Poland	£3.57	22.6%	£4.33	21.0%
Europe	**£132.05**	**18.4%**	**£156.67**	**18.4%**

Source: Figures from Centre for Retail Research, http://www.retailresearch.org/onlineretailing.php

ONLINE SHOPPING

ACTIVITY…

Use the information in the table opposite to answer the following:
- Which country had the highest percentage of growth in 2014?
- Which country had the highest percentage of growth in 2015?
- Which country had the highest percentage of growth between 2014 and 2015?
- What percentage of total online sales did the UK generate in 2015?

Advantages of shopping online
- Available 24 hours a day, 7 days a week.
- Can purchase products from the comfort of your own home.
- Wide range of products are available from around the world.
- Special discounts are often available online.
- Easy to compare prices of products from a range of different places.
- Helps avoid the stress of a busy shops, travel, parking etc.

Disadvantages of online shopping
- Security issues (eg Internet or payment card fraud).
- Don't get to handle the product before purchasing it.
- May be extra costs associated with the purchase (eg delivery, postage).
- Don't get the product immediately and delivery can be slow during holiday periods.
- Limited personal contact and customer service.

How to stay safe online

Try not to make online purchases in a public place – You can't always guarantee that the network is secure. It is better to make these purchases on your home computer if possible.

Use safe payment options – Make sure the website link is legitimate and secure before you insert your payment details. Check the website address begins with 'https' or the padlock symbol. Some sites will allow you to use a 'middle-man' website, such as PayPal, which passes your payment onto the seller without them seeing your card details.

Protect your personal details – Don't share your password or login details with anyone. When making a card payment, you will never be asked for your pin or online banking password by a legitimate website.

Be wary of emails asking for your information – No legitimate website or even your bank will ask you for your pin number or online banking password via email.

FOR DISCUSSION…
- How does online shopping affect local shops and businesses?
- Discuss both the positive and the negative impacts.

INDEPENDENT LIVING

32. Budgeting

We are learning about:
- Needs and wants
- Income and expenditure
- Budgeting

CORE COMPETENCE
By the age of 14 pupils should "…compare the cost of food when planning to eat or cook at home."

Needs and wants
Needs are the basic things that we must have to survive, such as food, water, shelter and clothing. Wants are the things we would like to have to make our lives more comfortable, such as mobile phones, designer jeans and holidays abroad. As responsible consumers, we should be aware of our needs and wants, as it shows us how much money we spend on essential and non-essentials items.

THINK ABOUT… (TPD SM)
- Think about the products and services you have purchased recently.
- Write down 3 products or services that you needed and 3 others that you simply wanted.

Income and expenditure
Income is the money we earn or receive (going in) and expenditure is the money we spend (going out). Here are some examples:

Income	Expenditure
Job wages	Food
Benefits	Clothes
Lottery win	Household expenses

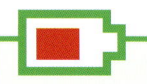

ACTIVITY… (TPD)
Think of 2 examples of incomes and 3 examples of expenditures not listed in the table above.

DID YOU KNOW?
According to the Office of National Statistics, UK households spent an average of £517 per week in 2013. The largest expenditure categories were housing (excluding mortgages); fuel and power; transport; and recreation and culture.

Source: Adapted from data from the Office for National Statistics licensed under the Open Government Licence v.3.0.

Budgeting
Budgeting is a good way to manage money effectively. A budget is a plan of the estimated money earned (income) and spent (expenditure) by someone over a set amount of time. It is basically a list of all the money we have going into and out of our accounts, and what is left over (disposable income).

Disposable income
This is the amount of money we have left to spend after expenses have been paid.

If we total our income and total our expenditure, we can work out our disposable income:

total income − total expenditure
= disposable income

This is very useful as it tells us how much money we have available to spend or save.

BUDGETING

Example of a monthly budget:

Income	Expenditure
Wage £1500	Food £450
Benefits £150	Clothes £150
Lottery win £50	Household expenses (including rent) £600
Total income £1700	**Total expenditure** £1200

Disposable income (total income – total expenditure) £500

FOR DISCUSSION…
Working in a group, discuss various ways that a family could reduce their monthly expenditure.

ACTIVITY…
Think of a product or service that you want.
- How long would it take you to save for that product or service?
- Can you think of any ways that you could reduce your spending to save for your product sooner?

EXTENSION ACTIVITY…
Keep a budget for a week.
Record the following:
- Your income (eg allowance)
- Your expenditure (eg sweets, clothes)
- Your disposable income (the money left over at the end of the week)

PRACTICAL
- Plan a healthy dish for a family of 4 that costs under £5.
- Your meal should reflect both the Eatwell Guide and the 8 tips.

PRACTICAL
Plan a sweet and sour sauce.
Record the price of the ingredients for your sauce.
Compare the cost to:
- a jar of sweet and sour sauce
- a portion of sweet and sour sauce from a local takeaway

Comment on your findings.

INDEPENDENT LIVING

33. Super savers

We are learning about:
- The importance of managing our money effectively
- The consequences of not managing our money effectively
- How we can manage our money effectively

The importance of managing our money effectively

It is important we learn how to manage our money effectively so we can take responsibility for our finances and avoid debt or bankruptcy.

> **Debt** – is money that is owed or due.
>
> **Bankruptcy** – is the legal status of a person who is unable to pay back their debts. If a person is declared as bankrupt, their assets (valuable goods) are usually sold to pay off some of the debt. By the end of the process, their debts are cleared but they may find it difficult to get a loan in the future.

The consequences of not managing our money effectively

Difficulty paying the bills, increasing debts from loans and credit cards, and having to cut back on essential items such as food are all signs that we are not managing our money effectively. This can have some serious impacts on our health, relationships and accommodation:

Health – Financial difficulty is a common cause of stress. Symptoms can include anxiety, feeling sick, headaches, trouble sleeping and even depression. Extended periods of stress can have a negative impact on both our physical and mental health.

Relationships – Financial difficulty can put a lot of strain on relationships. Anxiety can cause short tempers and arguments, and individuals can become so distracted by their money troubles that they don't have as much time for their friends and family.

Accommodation – If we fall behind on rent payments we could be evicted. If we cannot pay our mortgage instalments, we could lose our home and all the money we invested in it. It may also be difficult to get future accommodation or mortgages.

> **THINK ABOUT…**
> Can you think of any other consequences of poor money management?

How we can manage our money effectively

Budgeting – Make a plan of our estimated income (money coming in) and expenditure (money going out). We can then work out our disposable income (income – expenditure) to see what money we have available to spend. If our expenditure is higher than our income or we don't have much disposable income left over, we will need to look at ways to cut back on our expenses.

SUPER SAVERS

Save money regularly – Putting money aside for holidays, birthday and Christmas presents, large purchases or unplanned expenses is a good habit to get into. It means we can afford larger expenses and any unplanned costs.

Be responsible with credit cards – Credit cards are a useful way to spread purchase payments but it can be tempting to spend more than we can afford to repay. Unfortunately if we do not meet our repayments we will be charged interest, pay out more money and can get ourselves into debt.

THINK ABOUT... (TPD, SM)
- Why is it important for children to learn how to manage money?
- Can you think of any ways to get children to develop this skill?

ACTIVITY... (TPD, SM)
Make a list of 5 common things that people save for.

ACTIVITY... (WO, TPD, BC)
- Working in a group, come up with as many saving tips as you can think of.
- Decide on the top 5 tips and create a poster to display them.

ACTIVITY... (MI, TPD)
- List 3 high street banks.
- Why is it a good idea to save money in a bank?

EXTENSION ACTIVITY... (WO, TPD, MI, SM)
Class Survey

Conduct a survey to find out:
- How many people in your class have a bank account?
- Which bank do they save their money in?
- What type of account do they have?

RESEARCH ACTIVITY... (MI, TPD, SM)
Choose 1 high street bank.

Investigate 3 different types of account it offers. Find out:
- What makes each account different.
- The advantages and disadvantages of each.

69

INDEPENDENT LIVING

34. Methods of payment

We are learning about:
- Different methods of payment
- Advantages and disadvantages of a range of payment options

There are many ways that we can pay for goods and services. It is important that we learn about the advantages and disadvantages of a range of payment methods so that we can choose the most suitable options for us.

Method of payment	Advantages	Disadvantages
Cash	• Quick and convenient, without any further processing to be done. • May get discount.	• Risk of loss or theft. • May overspend, as it can be tempting to spend all the cash in one go.
Cheque	• Don't have to carry large amounts of cash about, avoiding the risk of loss or theft.	• Declining method of payment. • Not used in many shops anymore. • Need a bank account.
Credit card	• Items can be bought and paid for later or over a longer period of time. • Payment protection on single items costing £100 or over.	• May overspend. We can spend more than we have, as we are borrowing money and don't need to have the funds in a bank account. • Can end up paying more for the purchase (the interest*) if the balance is not paid by the due date. • Interest rates can be high if the balance isn't paid within a set (usually short) period of time. • There may be a maximum amount of money you can spend. This is known as a credit limit.
Debit card	• Don't have to carry large amounts of cash about, avoiding the risk of loss or theft. • Easy to use. • Money is taken directly from the bank account.	• May overspend. If there is an overdraft set up on the account then we can spend more than what we have. • Need a bank account.
Loan	• Items may be bought and paid for later or over a longer period of time.	• Often we will pay more for the purchase in return for the convenience of paying it off over a period of time.
Hire purchase	• Items may be bought and paid for later or over a longer period of time.	• We don't own the item until the final payment is paid. • Like a loan, we will often pay more for the purchase in return for the convenience of paying it off over a period of time.
In-store card	• Items may be bought and paid for later or over a longer period of time. • Discount may be offered. • Loyalty points may be offered.	• Can only use the card in the store it is issued in. • Like a credit card, we can end up paying more for the purchase if the balance is not paid by the due date. • Interest rates can be high if the balance isn't paid within a set (usually short) period of time. • There may be a maximum amount of money you can spend. This is known as a credit limit.

METHODS OF PAYMENT

* Interest – This is a fee charged for borrowing money or delaying payment of a debt. The fee is usually calculated as a percentage of the sum borrowed. This is known as the interest rate.

APR – stands for Annual Percentage Rate. It is the actual rate that is charged for borrowing (or by investing) money.

THINK ABOUT... [TPD] [BC]

- What do you think the most popular payment method will be in 10 years' time?
- Imagine life in 50 years' time, what might our payment methods be then?

ACTIVITY... [TPD] [SM]

Suggest a suitable method of payment for each of the items listed below:

- Weekly food shopping
- A new car
- A new sofa
- A new outfit (eg jeans and a top)

Give reasons for your answer.

35. Legislation

We are learning about:
- What legislation exists to protect consumers

There are special laws (legislation) that protect us as consumers if we encounter problems with products or services. It is important we learn about the different legislation that exists to protect us so we can become more responsible consumers. It is also important that we keep up to date with current legislation because it is often revised.

Consumer Rights Act 2015

The following legislation has been consolidated and updated to form the Consumer Rights Act 2015:

- Supply of Goods (Implied Terms) Act 1973
- Sale of Goods Act 1979
- Supply of Goods and Services Act 1982
- Sale and Supply of Goods Act 1994
- Sale and Supply of Goods to Consumers Regulations 2002
- Unfair Contract Terms Act 1977
- Unfair Terms in Consumer Contracts Regulations 1999

DID YOU KNOW?

The Consumer Rights Act came into force on 1 October 2015. The Act updates and improves consumer law. It sets out a simple, modern framework of consumer rights.

The core rights of the Consumer Rights Act are:

- *The right to get what you pay for.*
- *The right that goods and digital content are fit for purpose and services are provided with reasonable care and skill.*
- *The right to have faults in your purchases rectified free of charge, or to be provided with a refund or replacement.*

Goods contracts

What statutory rights are there under a goods contract?

- Goods must be of satisfactory quality, ie free of defects, made to a good finish, safe and durable.

- Goods must be fit for purpose, ie goods should do what they promise or are advertised to do, or as told to you by the trader.

- Goods must be as described, ie they match the sample provided, conform to the label, advert or verbal description.

- Goods must also be installed correctly if that is part of the contract. For example, a new wall-mounted flatscreen TV should be securely fastened to its wall brackets and connected up to the customer's cable, satellite or other provider.

What happens if these rights are not met?

If goods do not meet the conditions of the statutory rights, depending on the circumstances, we may be entitled to a repair, replacement or refund. If we have had the goods a while and have been using them, some money may be deducted from the refund.

Digital content contracts

Digital contracts are for intangible goods. These are goods that cannot be touched. Often they are goods that we own but are stored and processed from a distance by the trader and supplied in digital form (eg downloaded games, apps and e-books) and transmitted to your phone, tablet or computer.

What statutory rights are there under a digital content contract?

Occasionally the digital content we purchase can corrupt or disrupt the functioning of another device or content. If this happens, depending on the circumstances, we may have the right to have the damaged equipment or content repaired by the trader or to receive compensation.

Service contracts

Services are also intangible. They are provided by suppliers and traders such as builders, mechanics, hairdressers, waiters and wedding photographers.

What statutory rights are there under a service contract?

- The service must be carried out with reasonable care and skill.

- If the timescale and cost has not been agreed in advance, the service must be carried out within a reasonable time and charged at a reasonable cost.

- If you receive unsatisfactory service the trader must put things right at no extra cost to you. Depending on the circumstances you may be entitled to the service being carried out again, or, if that is not possible, a price reduction.

Consumer Contracts Regulations (Information, Cancellation and Additional Charges) 2013

This is another important piece of legislation that we should learn about. It replaces the Distance Selling Regulations and applies to items bought online, at a distance or away from a trader's premises (eg at home).

Key facts:

- A trader can no longer charge you for additional items added by a pre-ticked box online.

- You can cancel a service contract online (eg a gym membership) 14 days after you enter it.

- You should get a refund within 14 days of cancelling goods or services online or within 14 days of returning the goods to the trader.

Regardless of where we buy goods and services (eg in-store or online), the following information must be given:

LEGISLATION

- a description of the goods or service.
- the total price of the goods or service.
- cost of delivery and details of who pays for the cost of returning items if you cancel and change your mind.
- details of any right to cancel. The trader also needs to provide, or make available, a standard cancellation form to make cancelling easy (although you don't have to use it).
- information about the seller, including their geographical address and phone number.
- information on the compatibility of digital content with hardware and other software.

(Adapted from: http://www.which.co.uk/consumer-rights/regulation/consumer-contracts-regulations)

EXTENSION ACTIVITY…

- Read the case study below.
- Research the Consumer Contracts Regulations (Information, Cancellation and Additional Charges) 2013 legislation and identify 3 pieces of information that the trader must include in the written contract with Patricia.

CASE STUDY

Patricia has made an off-premises contract (at home) for new double-glazing.

When we are NOT entitled to statutory rights

- If you change your mind (unless bought online, by catalogue, shopping channel etc where you have a 14 days cooling-off period).
- If you don't follow the care or installation instructions correctly.
- If you use the product for the wrong purpose.
- If you try to fix the fault yourself before notifying the trader and giving them a chance to put things right.
- If the problem was pointed out to you prior to purchase.
- If the problem has occurred due to fair wear and tear or accidental damage.

RESEARCH ACTIVITY…

Read the case studies below and carry out your own research to find out the following:
- What legislation exists to protect each consumer?
- How are they protected?
- What advice would you give them?

CASE STUDY 1

Rachel was shopping and she chose a new dress for a party she was going to. When she got home she decided she didn't like the colour anymore.

CASE STUDY 2

Laura and Andrew were eating at their favourite restaurant. That night, Andrew was very sick. His friends, who were at the same restaurant, also said they were sick soon after their meal.

CASE STUDY 3

Jane bought a DVD. When she was watching it she noticed that the quality wasn't good and some parts of the film were missing. She thought it may have been a copy or a fake.

CASE STUDY 4

Philippa downloaded a retro game app for her tablet and paid £25.00. The game was not what she expected based on the promotional information and was very basic for what she paid for it.

CASE STUDY 5

Zara bought a new car from a local trader. A week later things started to go wrong. Her car brakes wouldn't work.

CASE STUDY 6

Mark purchased and downloaded a software update to his computer. It was supposed to allow him to edit and add special effects to his photographs but when he started to use the software it caused his computer to keep crashing.

INDEPENDENT LIVING

36. Making a complaint

We are learning about:
- Why consumers complain
- How to resolve complaints
- How to write a letter of complaint

It is important we learn what to do if we encounter a problem with a product or service. If we understand our rights as consumers and complain effectively, the situation can hopefully be resolved.

Why consumers complain

There are many reasons why consumers may complain but some of the most common reasons are listed below.

The products or services:

- are faulty.
- are dangerous.
- are not fit for purpose.
- are not of a satisfactory quality.
- do not match their description.

ACTIVITY...

- Give everyone in your class a post it or strip of paper.
- Ask everyone to write down 1 complaint either they or a family member have had about a product or service.
- Collect the post its and record everyone's complaints on the board.
- Add up all the complaints that are the same and create a list of 'The Top 5 Complaints'.

How to resolve complaints

- Know the legislation that protects you as consumers.
- Understand your consumer rights and responsibilities.
- Contact the appropriate consumer organisation (eg Citizens Advice) if you need further help or guidance.

How to write a letter of complaint

Basic rules
- Keep your letter short and to the point.
- List events in the order they happened and include dates if you can.
- Keep to the facts. Don't make allegations or accusations that you're unable to prove.
- Never use abusive or offensive language.

A complaint letter should include the following information:

- your name, address and contact number.
- the name and address of the trader.
- customer or reference number.
- the date you bought or ordered the item or service.
- what you bought and the make or model number.
- how much you paid and how you paid for the item or service (method of payment).
- a description of the fault or problem.
- anything that was agreed at the time you bought the item or service.
- brief details of any conversations you've already had about the problem.
- what you want the trader to do. For example, a refund, replacement, repair or compensation.
- a reminder of what legal consumer rights you have.
- a date by when you want the trader to reply.
- what you will do next if you have not heard from the trader by this date.
- copies of any paperwork you can use as evidence.

Source: Citizens Advice, http://www.adviceguide.org.uk/england/consumer_e/consumer_taking_ action_e/consumer_making_a_complaint_e/consumer_dealing_with_the_trader_e/written_ complaint_about_a_trader_checklist.htm

MAKING A COMPLAINT

Sample letter

Hair Supplies
110 High Street
Woodville
WT23 8RT

Veronica O'Loane
5 Wood Lane
Woodville
WT20 9HQ
Tel: 242 80527296

21 November 2015

Complaint about faulty goods

Dear Sir or Madam,

I bought a set of hair straighteners from you on 17 November 2015. I paid £150 in cash for them.

I now find the goods have the following fault:

The straighteners stop working after 1 minute. When I turn them off and on again they will not start again for 30 minutes.

Under the Consumer Rights Act 2015, goods you supply must be fit for purpose. As there was a problem with the goods when I bought them, I request that you repair the goods at no cost to me.

I have enclosed a copy of the receipt in support of my claim.

Please respond within 14 days of receiving this letter or I will have to take appropriate further action.

Yours faithfully

Veronica O'Loane

Veronica O'Loane

DID YOU KNOW?

If a consumer simply changes their mind about goods they bought, by law they're not entitled to a refund. However, shops will often provide a goodwill gesture such as a refund within 28 days, a credit note or an exchange.

This does not affect your statutory rights
During a sale, shops often reduce these goodwill gestures but consumers still have all of the same rights when it comes to faulty or misdescribed goods.

RESEARCH ACTIVITY...

Research the following policies from 3 different shops:

   a) refunds
   b) returns

- Record your findings.
- Comment on your findings and recommend any improvements you can think of.

75

INDEPENDENT LIVING

37. Consumer Organisations

We are learning about:
- A range of consumer organisations
- How consumer organisations help protect us as consumers

There is a wide range of organisations that exist to protect us as consumers. It is important we learn about them so that we know which one to turn to if we need advice, support or guidance about a consumer related issue.

Citizens Advice
Website: http://www.citizensadvice.co.uk

Citizens Advice is the largest advice charity in Northern Ireland. As an advice and information service, it:

- works against poverty.
- meets the information and advice needs of over 95,000 people per year in member bureaux.
- has over 320,000 people viewing more than 2.2 million topics online via Adviceguide.
- provides advice from 28 offices across Northern Ireland.

The service helps people resolve their debt, benefits, housing, legal, discrimination, employment, immigration, consumer and other problems. Its services are available to everyone regardless of race, gender, sexuality, age, nationality, disability or religion.

The principles of Citizens Advice:

- *Free* – no one has to pay for any part of the service.
- *Impartial* – Citizens Advice doesn't judge clients or make assumptions. Their service is open to everyone and they treat everyone equally.
- *Confidential* – Citizens Advice won't pass on anything a client tells them without their permission.
- *Independent* – Citizens Advice always act in the interests of their clients without influence from any outside bodies.

The Consumer Council for Northern Ireland
Website: http://www.consumercouncil.org.uk

The Consumer Council was set up by Government in 1985 and is funded by the Department of Enterprise, Trade and Investment (DETI). Their job is to:

- speak up for consumers and give them a voice.
- ensure that the policy makers in Northern Ireland hear that voice and take it into account when they are making decisions that affect us all.

They do this by running information and education campaigns, influencing the public and private sectors, undertaking research and producing publications. They also help individual consumers with issues and complaints about buses, trains, planes, ferries, natural gas, electricity, coal, postal services and water.

The Northern Ireland Trading Standards Service
Website: http://www.detini.gov.uk/deti-consumer-index

The role of the Trading Standards Service is to:

- promote and maintain fair trading.
- protect consumers.
- enable reputable businesses to thrive within Northern Ireland.

They do this by enforcing a wide range of consumer legislation in order to protect consumers and honest businesses. They will also give advice to businesses in order to help them comply with the law.

CONSUMER ORGANISATIONS

Consumerline
Website: http://www.nidirect.gov.uk/consumerline

Consumerline is a telephone and online advice service for Northern Ireland.

The telephone advisors listen to each caller's query and provide clear, practical advice on a wide range of consumer issues. If it is appropriate they will forward details of the complaint to the Trading Standards Service for investigation.

CASE STUDY 2
Hannah's train has been delayed three times this week. She approached a member of staff about this and was unhappy with the service she received.

CASE STUDY 3
Brendan needs some legal advice about a recent issue he has experienced. He is worried his solicitors will charge him for their time.

RESEARCH ACTIVITY...
Working in a group, research 1 consumer organisation that we haven't looked at already.

Create a leaflet informing young adults about the consumer organisation.

Include information on the following:
- The organisation's history and background
- How the organisation protects consumers
- Key areas of its work
- Its contact details
- Images or illustrations

ACTIVITY...
Read the case studies that follow.

What consumer organisations would you advise these people to contact for help? Give reasons for your answer.

CASE STUDY 1
Conor is trying to set up a business of his own. He wants to ensure he is following all the correct rules and legislation.

HOME ECONOMICS
HOME AND FAMILY LIFE

HOME AND FAMILY LIFE

38. Different Types of Family

We are learning about:
- What makes each family different
- Family structures

Families are unique in many ways. Families can be:

- Different sizes
- Made up of different parents
- Made up of a mix of people from other families

It is important we learn about these differences so we can understand and respect other people's backgrounds.

THINK ABOUT... [TPD] [SM]
How is your family different from some of your friends' families? What is it that makes them different?

Family Structures

Nuclear family – A family made up of two parents and their children.

Extended family – This includes cousins, aunts and uncles, and grandparents.

Lone/single parent family – A single parent family (could be a mother or a father).

Foster family – A temporary arrangement when someone else looks after a child and acts as their parent/guardian.

Adopted family – This is a permanent, legal arrangement. A person who adopts a child becomes legally responsible for the child.

Step family – This is a family where at least one parent has a child from another relationship.

DID YOU KNOW?
- Within the UK, 25% of all families with dependent children are single parent families.
- This percentage has remained the same since 2001 but increased significantly from just 8% in 1971.

Source: Figures from Gingerbread, http://www.gingerbread.org.uk/content/365/Statistics

THINK ABOUT... [MI] [TPD]
Why do you think the number of single parent families has increased since 1971?

ACTIVITY... [MI] [TPD]
Explain how adoption is different from fostering.

RESEARCH ACTIVITY... [MI] [TPD] [ICT] [COM]
- Create your own family tree.
- Include the names of your extended family and go back as far as you can.
- You may have to ask some family members to help you.

RESEARCH ACTIVITY... [MI] [TPD] [ICT] [COM]
Research some famous families.

Write down an example for each of the following family structures. The first one has been completed for you:

- Nuclear (eg The Simpsons)
- Extended
- Lone/single parent
- Foster
- Adopted
- Step

PRACTICAL [BC] [MI] [TPD] [SM] [MA]
The Perrys are a large family. They are organising a special lunch and want to invite cousins, aunts and uncles, and grandparents. Plan and prepare a suitable lunch for the extended family.

80

ROLES AND RESPONSIBILITIES

39. Roles and Responsibilities

We are learning about:
- The responsibilities people may have within their family
- The roles people play in their family
- How to become more involved in family life

It is important we learn about other people's roles and responsibilities within their families so we can understand and respect their backgrounds. It might also show us ways to become more involved in our own family life.

Responsibilities

There are many tasks that need completed every day to make family life run smoothly. For example:

- Shopping
- Cleaning
- Ironing
- Cooking
- Driving
- DIY
- Gardening

It would take one person a long time to do all of these tasks. However, if the tasks were shared between two or more people, they could be completed much faster.

A lot of families share these tasks between the parents, who have the responsibility of looking after their children and their home. As we get older, we might also be asked to complete or take on some of these tasks, making them our responsibility.

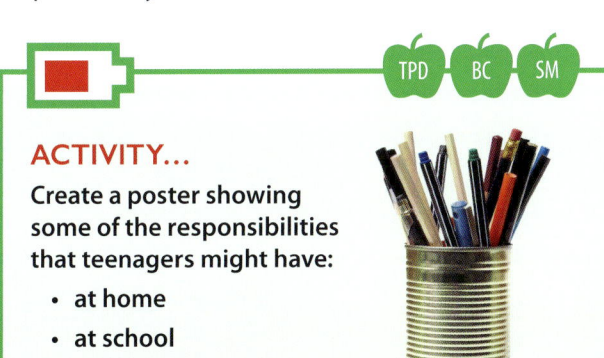

ACTIVITY...

Create a poster showing some of the responsibilities that teenagers might have:
- at home
- at school
- in their community

ACTIVITY...

- List 3 jobs or tasks that you could do each day to help your family and home life.
- List the top 5 responsibilities you think a parent has.

Roles

A role is the part that a person plays. Family members all have unique roles to play, as fathers, mothers, sons, daughters and siblings. Traditionally:

- fathers took on the role of 'breadwinner', bringing in money and providing for the family.
- mothers took on the role of 'homemaker', coordinating the household tasks, caring for the children and preparing food for the family.
- sons were expected to help the father with manual tasks.
- daughters were expected to help their mother with the household tasks.

Today, these roles are not so clearly defined and they often depend on individual skills and qualities.

Stereotyping is when people have a fixed view or opinion about a person or thing. For example, some people think that women should do the cleaning and make the dinner, and that men should earn the money for their family.

Role reversal is when a person's traditional role is reversed or swapped. For example, instead of the mother staying at home to look after the children and the father going to work to earn the money, the mother goes to work and the father stays at home.

81

HOME AND FAMILY LIFE

Shared roles are when roles are divided between two or more people. For example, two parents share earning money, the household jobs and caring for the children.

THINK ABOUT... [SM] [TPD]
- Can you think of any other examples of stereotypes?
- How do these stereotypes make you feel?
- Can you think of 3 examples of shared roles within families?

ACTIVITY... [MI] [TPD] [SM]
Read the case study below.
- How have families changed from Mary's day?
- What changes in society have caused this?

CASE STUDY

Back in Mary's day...
"Back in my day, the fathers went out to work and provided for the family. The mothers stayed at home, did the housework, washed the clothes, cooked the dinner and looked after the children. Us girls helped our mothers and the boys did any manual labour or outside chores. Nowadays things are quite different!"

ACTIVITY... [TPD] [SM]
If everyone takes greater responsibility for the roles that they play within their family it makes living together easier.

Create a table showing:
- all the roles that the members of your family have.
- all the responsibilities that the members of your family have.

EXTENSION ACTIVITY... [MI] [TPD] [SM]
- Looking at your table, are the roles and responsibilities divided equally among your family members?
- If you find that some family members do more than others, are there any roles or responsibilities that could be given to another family member to help them?

THINK ABOUT... [TPD] [SM]
Why do you think it is important for parents or guardians to set a good example?

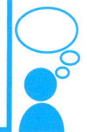

EXTENSION ACTIVITY... [MI] [TPD] [SM] [COM] [ICT]
Create a family manual, showing everyone's roles and responsibilities.

It should include the following information:
- A photograph of your family.
- The names of each family member.
- A description of each family member.
- A description of a typical day in your family.
- A rota showing the roles and responsibilities of each family member for one day.
- A weekly dinner menu for your family.

PRACTICAL [BC] [WO] [TPD] [SM]
Plan a typical evening meal for your family.

82

DEALING WITH CONFLICT

40. Dealing with conflict

We are learning about:
- The causes of family conflict
- Strategies to resolve conflict

Everyone can't agree with each other all of the time. Disagreements are part of every day life, particularly among people that are close to each other, such as families. Many families experience conflict but how each family chooses to deal with disagreements can be very different. It is important we learn how to manage conflict effectively so that our relationships are happy and healthy.

THINK ABOUT...
- Think about what makes a family happy.
- Create a list of 5 factors that you think are important.
- Rank your list from 1–5, with 1 being the most important and 5 the least.

The causes of family conflict

Stress – Stress is one of the most common causes of family conflict. Its symptoms (including anxiety, tiredness and even depression) often affect people's mood and patience, causing them to react more negatively to situations than if they were relaxed.

Money problems – Financial worries can put a lot of strain on family life, causing short tempers, arguments and stress.

Work – Job pressures, responsibilities, heavy workloads and long hours can all limit the time that people have to spend with their families. They are also all causes of stress, which can affect the quality of the time that families do get to spend together.

Ill health – Most people will become anxious and stressed if a close family member is unwell. Caring for or visiting this family member can also leave less time to spend with other family members.

Sibling rivalry – When brothers and sisters argue or compete for their parents' attention, this can cause tension within the whole family.

THINK ABOUT...
How does arguing with someone make you feel?

Strategies to resolve conflict

Prevention – Stop the conflict from arising in the first place.

Stay calm – Don't raise your voice or say anything unkind.

Listen – It's important to listen to the other person's opinion and try to understand how they feel.

Compromise – Try and meet the other person halfway.

Apologise – It might be difficult to say you're sorry but it's often the fastest way to stop an argument.

ACTIVITY...
- Explain 2 common causes of conflict.
- Why is compromise an effective way to resolve conflict?
- What are your top 3 tips for resolving conflict?

EXTENSION ACTIVITY...
Design a help sheet for parents titled 'Living with teenagers'.
Include the following information:
- 3 examples of common disagreements within families.
- The cause of each conflict from a) the teenager's and b) the parents' point of view.
- Possible solutions for each conflict.

ACTIVITY...
Read the case studies that follow.
Identify:
- the conflict in each case.
- the cause(s) of each conflict.
- how the conflict could be resolved.

83

HOME AND FAMILY LIFE

CASE STUDY 1

Lucia is three and is a handful to take shopping! On many occasions she has screamed loudly when her mummy said no to buying sweets. At playschool, Lucia often refuses to share her toys with the other children. At home, she won't tidy up her toys and sometimes she throws her food around at dinnertime. This is causing a lot of stress at home and Lucia's brother and sister complain that she gets all the attention from their parents.

CASE STUDY 2

Matthew is 13 and likes to get his own way! He is huffing with his parents at the moment because they said he has to be home before 9.00 pm on a school night. Matthew thinks this isn't fair because some of his friends are allowed to stay out until later. Matthew has been getting in trouble at school recently because he has missed several homeworks and his teachers and parents are worried that his attitude has changed. This is causing a lot of anxiety and tension at home.

CASE STUDY 3

Angela is a mother of three children and she works full time. Her husband Zac works away from home and Angela works night shifts so that she is there during the day to look after her children. At night Angela's mother or niece stays with the children. Recently Angela has found it difficult to manage and has had to take time off work due to sickness twice this month. She has been getting cross at silly things recently and has been snapping at her children. She rarely gets time to eat her own dinner because she is so busy looking after her children. All this is making her upset and she feels like she can't cope anymore.

41. Parenting

We are learning about:
- The skills and qualities of a good parent

Parents influence us in many ways. It is important we learn about the qualities of a good parent to help us gain a deeper understanding of this important family role. Parenting skills evolve gradually through experience and there is no definitive guide as to what makes the 'perfect parent'; it all depends on the needs of each child.

The qualities of a good parent

Patience – It is important for parents to take time to listen to their children and address any problems calmly, without becoming annoyed or anxious.

Understanding – it is important for parents to consider their children's feelings and try to see things from their perspective. This will help their children feel loved and secure.

Communication – It is important for parents to take time to talk to their children, not just when they are giving instructions or providing discipline. When parents are interested and listen, their children will feel valued.

PARENTING

Consistency – It is important for parents to be fair and set rules that they can stick to. Children like to know where the stand and find it difficult if they are allowed to do something one day but not the next day, or if one parent says yes and the other says no.

Affection – It is important for parents to show their children love and affection to fulfil their emotional needs. This love makes children feel wanted and safe, and is especially important during the early stages of childhood.

Responsibility – It is important for parents to take responsibility for the influential role that they play in their children's lives. They must set a good example, displaying the attitudes and values that they would like to see in their children.

Recognition – It is important for parents to recognise and reward good behaviour. Praise develops children's self-esteem and self-confidence.

Discipline – It is important for parents to discipline their children so that they learn:

- the difference between right and wrong
- how to protect themselves from danger
- what is socially acceptable

Discipline is not all about parents shouting and getting their own way. Recognising and rewarding positive behaviour is often much more effective than negative discipline such as criticism and guilt.

ACTIVITY...
- List 5 qualities that a good parent might show.
- Rank these qualities in order of importance.
- Explain why each quality is important.

ACTIVITY...
Design a reward chart for a toddler. Include the following information:
- What the toddler will be rewarded for.
- The type of rewards the toddler will receive.

ACTIVITY...
Read the following post from David, a soon-to-be parent, on an online parenting forum.
- Imagine you are the parent of a 12 month old child.
- Write a reply comment to David, offering advice and reassurance.
- You could include information on:
   a) The role of a parent
   b) The qualities of a good parent

PARENTING PALS

I recently found out that I'm going to be a dad. I'm a bit overwhelmed and worried that I won't make a good parent! My partner is also very anxious. We have been together for many years. Can anyone give me any advice?
– David

HOME AND FAMILY LIFE

42. Changing needs of family members

We are learning about:
- Basic needs
- How these needs change throughout life

We all have a range of basic needs, which change throughout life. It is important we learn about these needs to ensure that our own are met and to help other people achieve theirs.

Basic needs

Physical needs – These are the things our bodies need to live in good health, such as food, clothing and shelter.

Intellectual needs – These are the things we need to develop learning, such as stimulation, communication, education and play.

Emotional needs – These are the things we need to feel safe and accepted, such as affection, acknowledgement and security.

Social needs – These are the things we need to feel connected to other people, such as friendship, communication and support.

Needs throughout life

The table opposite shows some of our physical, intellectual, emotional and social needs throughout life. Many of our needs remain with us as we progress through each stage of the life cycle but some needs are unique for particular stages.

THINK ABOUT…
Consider the consequences of not achieving each of your basic needs.
For example, if your emotional needs were not met, how would this affect you?

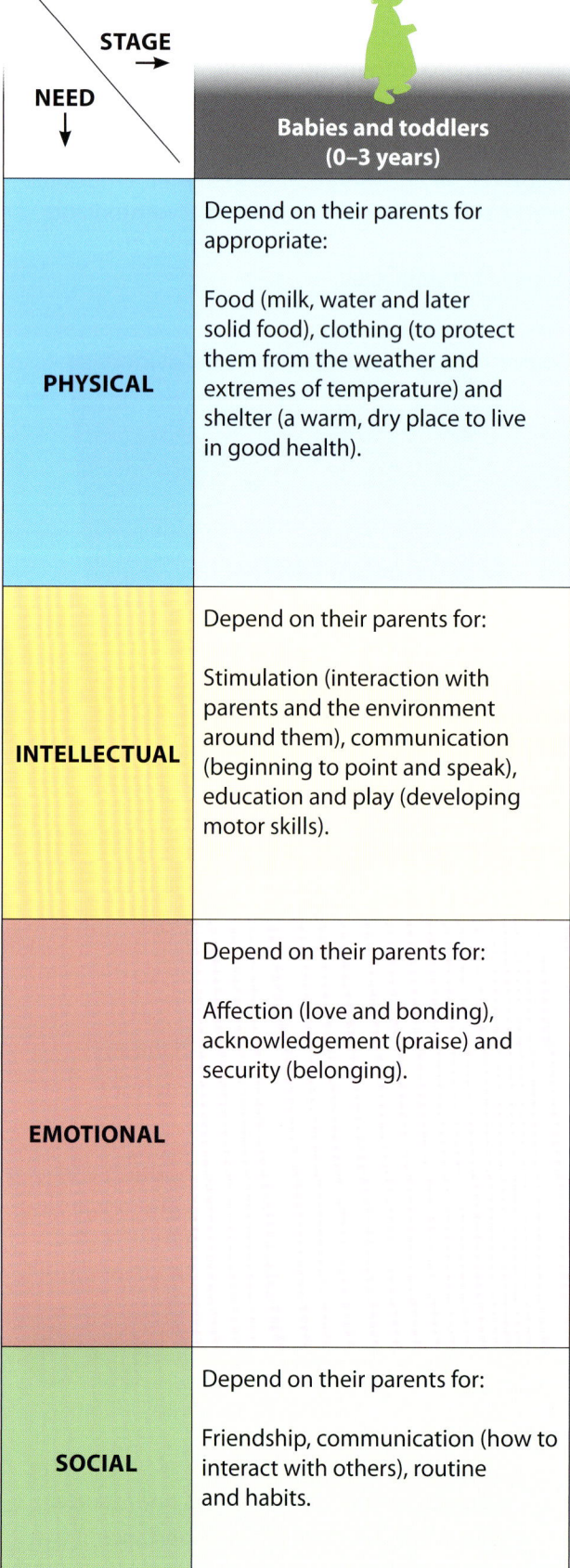

NEED ↓ / STAGE →	Babies and toddlers (0–3 years)
PHYSICAL	Depend on their parents for appropriate: Food (milk, water and later solid food), clothing (to protect them from the weather and extremes of temperature) and shelter (a warm, dry place to live in good health).
INTELLECTUAL	Depend on their parents for: Stimulation (interaction with parents and the environment around them), communication (beginning to point and speak), education and play (developing motor skills).
EMOTIONAL	Depend on their parents for: Affection (love and bonding), acknowledgement (praise) and security (belonging).
SOCIAL	Depend on their parents for: Friendship, communication (how to interact with others), routine and habits.

CHANGING NEEDS OF FAMILY MEMBERS

Childhood (4–11 years)	Adolescence (12–18 years)	Adulthood (19–64 years)	Old age (65+)
Depend on their parents for: Food (high energy, protein and calcium is important), clothing and shelter.	Depend mostly on their parents for: Food (iron and protein is important), clothing and shelter.	Provide their own: Food, clothing and shelter.	If they are unable to provide their own physical needs, these may be catered for by family members or carers: Food (a healthy, balanced diet to fight off illness), clothing and shelter (may have to move into accommodation that provides suitable care).
Depend on their parents and friends for: Stimulation, communication (improving vocabulary and social skills), education and play (beginning to read, write and use number).	Stimulation, communication (improving language, written and social skills), education and play (developing reading, writing and number abilities).	Stimulation, communication and education (development of abilities throughout work and further education).	Stimulation, communication and education. It is important to keep the mind active at this stage. Sharing knowledge and experiences will help memory, which can decline with old age.
Depend on their parents and friends for: Affection, acknowledgement and security.	Adolescence can affect people's feelings and emotions, making the following needs even more important throughout this stage: Affection (friendships and relationships), acknowledgement (academic and sporting success) and security (belonging and stability).	Affection (from friends, partners and children), acknowledgement (feeling valued and respected) and security (stability).	Affection (from family and friends), acknowledgement (feeling valued, useful and respected), security and support (to cope with loss and bereavement).
Depend on their parents and friends for: Friendship and communication (developing interaction and behaviour skills).	Friendship and communication with people of a similar age are both very important throughout this stage.	Friendship, communication and support (with and from friends, family, the community and work colleagues).	During old age people tend to have fewer relationships so friendship, communication and support from family and friends becomes more important.

HOME AND FAMILY LIFE

ACTIVITY...

List 2 examples of each of the following basic needs:
- Physical
- Intellectual
- Emotional
- Social

EXTENSION ACTIVITY...

Below are the 5 stages of the life cycle:

- Babies and toddlers
- Childhood 
- Adolescence 
- Adulthood 
- Old age 

Choose 2 stages and explain how the basic needs can be met for each.

ACTIVITY...

Read the case studies opposite and answer the following questions.
- List 5 ways that Lucy is dependent on her parents for her basic needs.
- Explain 3 ways that Ben's parents could help develop his independence.
- Think of 1 toy that could help meet Seamus' intellectual needs. Explain how the toy will help him develop. You might want to use some of the following terms: stimulation, communication, education and play.

CASE STUDY 1

Lucy is 4 months old and depends on her parents to meet her needs.

CASE STUDY 2

Ben is an adolescent and complains he isn't given any freedom to make his own choices.

CASE STUDY 3

Seamus is 3 years old and has just started play school.

Copyright Information

Copyright has been acknowledged to the best of our ability. If there are any inadvertent errors or omissions, we shall be happy to correct them in any future editions.

Acknowledgements

Thanks to the following organisations and copyright holders for their kind permission to use their logos, titles, images and information:

> British Nutrition Foundation, Centre for Retail Research, Citizens Advice, Department of Enterprise Trade and Investment, Fairtrade Foundation, Food Standards Agency Northern Ireland, NHS Choices, Office for National Statistics, Soil Association, The Consumer Council for Northern Ireland, Unilever PLC and group companies

Licences

Some of the information on pages 22, 53 and 66 contains public sector information licensed under the Open Government Licence v3.0. A copy of this license can be viewed at: https://www.nationalarchives.gov.uk/doc/open-government-licence/version/3/

The image on page 61 is licensed under the Creative Commons Attribution 3.0 Unported License. Permission is granted to share and/or remix this work providing the work is attributed in the manner specified by the author or licensor. A copy of the license can be viewed at: https://creativecommons.org/licenses/by/3.0/

Picture Credits

All photographs are by iStockphoto except for the following which are included with kind permission of the copyright holders. The numbers denote page numbers.

> British Nutrition Foundation: 15 (top)
> Food Standards Agency Northern Ireland: 19 (bottom)
> P117: 61
> Public Health England: 22
> Rachel Irwin: 30 (all apart from bottom left)
> Rachel Robertson: 60
> Shutterstock: 32 (bottom), 38
> Unilever PLC and group companies: 8 (top)

The following tables, graphs and images are included with kind permission of the copyright holders.

> Department of Health: 53
> NHS Choices: 46 (left)
> Public Health England in association with the Welsh government, Food Standards Scotland and the Food Standards Agency in Northern Ireland: 22